Quaff 2006

PETER FORRESTAL is a freelance wine writer who lives in Perth. He is wine columnist for the local *Sunday Times*, contributes to national and international publications on wine and talks about wine regularly with John Clarke on ABC 'Statewide' in NSW. He was founding editor of *Australian Gourmet Traveller WINE*, and is the author, co-author or editor of 28 books, including the *Global Encyclopedia of Wine, Discover Australia: Wineries*, and *Margaret River*. He has judged at wine shows including the Sydney International Top 100 and the Concours Mondial de Bruxelles.

Quaff 2006

Peter Forrestal

Hardie Grant Books

Published in 2005
by Hardie Grant Books
85 High Street
Prahran, Victoria 3181, Australia
www.hardiegrant.com.au

ISBN 1 74066 347 0

Edited by Martine Lleonart
Cover design/photography and text design by Phil Campbell
Typesetting by Kirby Jones
Printed and bound in Australia by Griffin Press

1 3 5 7 9 10 8 6 4 2

In fond memory of Colin Climo (1953–2004).

Col was a talented wine writer,
and a meticulous, uncompromising journalist.
He was the best of pals.

And for those he left behind – his loving wife,
Dael, and son, Luke.

Contents

ACKNOWLEDGEMENTS   xi

BARGAIN HUNTER'S SURVIVAL GUIDE – AN INTRODUCTION
TO BUYING GREAT-VALUE-WINES   1
The Quaff 2006 Awards   4
Hall of Fame: The Reliables   8
How This Book Works   9
Vintage Reports: 2005–2001   12

CHEAP AND CHEERFUL – CASK WINES WORTH BUYING   15
White Casks   18
Red Casks   21
Fortified Casks   24

MORE THAN FROTH AND BUBBLE –
SPARKLING WINES UNDER $15   25
White Sparkling   29
Red Sparkling   33
Pink Bubbles   35
Sweet Sparkling   36

BOTTLED SUNSHINE – WHITE WINES UNDER $15   39
Chardonnay   40
Riesling   50
Sauvignon Blanc   57
Semillon   61
Verdelho and Other White Varietals   66
Semillon Chardonnay Blends   72
Semillon Sauvignon Blanc Blends   76
Other White Blends   82

PRETTY IN PINK – ROSES UNDER $15   87
Pink wines under $15   88

BARBECUE WINES – RED WINES UNDER $15   93
Cabernet Sauvignon   94
Merlot   99
Shiraz   106
Other Red Varietals   115
Cabernet Merlot Blends   121
Grenache Blends   128
Shiraz Cabernet Blends   132
Other Red Blends   137

KISSES SWEETER THAN WINE – SWEET WINES UNDER $15   143
Sweet Wines   146
Very Sweet Wines   148

GOOD ENOUGH FOR THE VICAR – FORTIFIED WINES UNDER $15   149
Port   152
Sherry   154
Muscat and Tokay   155

AN AFFAIR TO REMEMBER – IMPORTED WINES UNDER $20   157
Imported Sparkling   160
Imported Whites   162
Imported Reds   165

LASH OUT – GREAT-VALUE WINES OVER $15   169
Sparkling Wines over $15   172
White Wines over $15   173
Pink Wines over $15   179
Red Wines over $15   181
Sweet and Fortified Wines   194

HOW TO TRACK DOWN THE BARGAINS   197
Some Tips for the Bargain Hunter   199
Finding the Wines   202
Recommended Retailers   216
Wine Clubs and Online Retailers   229

DECODING THE JARGON – A QUICK WINE GLOSSARY   231

INDEX OF WINES   237

Acknowledgements

Claire Codrington is amazing: her wonderful organisational skills come to the fore as each edition of *Quaff* flows on and the deluge of tasting samples floods the office. There is no question that her thoughtfulness, careful planning and rigour make the tastings and the book possible. Christine de St Jorre has been a tower of strength helping to reduce the sheer volume of work and enabling Claire to survive the barrage of bottles. Proximity to the action means that Elaine Forrestal has been called on quite often enough – and, for that, and much more, I am grateful.

Once again, I thank Nevile Phillips for organising and running the Perth tastings with panache, savoir faire and ruthless efficiency. The poor showing of Collingwood and JJ's timidity since his marriage to Kate Lamont has meant that there has been little need this year for Nev to utter his usual rallying cry to action: 'Shut up, JJ'. I acknowledge the camaraderie of Nevile and colleagues Mike Adonis, Angus Barnes, Craig Drummond, John Jens, Diana Loots, Will Nairn, Wendy Roach and Nicole Walton around the tasting table at 1 Cobb Street.

Thanks to Ken Gargett, Louise Hemsley-Smith, Debby Irving, Gordon Melsom, Sophie Otton and Michele Round for help with keeping the book up-to-date.

I acknowledge the support of wine producers and wholesalers who, by supplying samples of their wines, provided the foundation on which the book was built. Our contacts at these wine companies have been unfailing cooperative and have frequently gone far beyond the call of duty.

In the spirit of the Quaff Awards, we announce that Southcorp's Debby Irving has won our 2006 'Dot the i's' Award for efficiency (that's two in a row, how reliable can one gal get!). Kristen Pryce of Peter Lehmann Wines is the winner of our long-service 'Codrington Medal' for having made Claire's life so much easier over so many years. **The Reliables:** Gabor Hernadi and Alex McPherson have been with us for all six editions of *Quaff*, while Margot De Bortoli and Paul Lenon have helped with five of the six editions.

We would also like to make a fuss over the following for their cheerful hard work on our behalf: Penny Agar, Sarah Angelini, Rebecca Ashmead, Beverley Atkinson, Gaby Barila, Angus Barnes, Michelle Barry, Hal Bibby, Mark Bolton, Narisha Boord, Julie Booth, Sarah Conway, Athena Corry, Bel Darley, Margot De Bortoli, Renee de Saxe, Maria-Teresa Di Mauro, Tarsha Edwards, Kathryn Fiorenza, Anna Gillman, Gabor Hernadi, Blair Hill, Rebecca Hopkins, Denys Hornabrook, Timothy Hunt, Debby Irving, Peter James, Emma Jane, Marcolina Jesus, Paul Lenon, Jenni Lockett, Hannah Lunnay, Graeme McDonough, Jayne McKennay, Kristin McLarty, Michael McNamara, Alex McPherson, Lloyd Meredith, Sandra Miranda, Michaela Murphy, Kim Neville, Tiffany Nugan, Dagmar O'Neill, Renae Power, Kristen Pryce, Matthew Redin, Brad Rey, Laura Rowe, Penny Salfinger, Branca Salaverry, Stephen Schrapel, Max Smeeth, Jeremy Stockman, Cherry Stowman, Matthew Tallentire, Virginia Taylor, Fiona Tiller, Lucinda Tippett, Dot Towler, Christina Tulloch, Katherine Ward, Jill Watson, Emily White, Jackie Whitehead, Anthony Woollams, Stacey Wood and Dale Wyman.

I am deeply appreciative of the support, encouragement and quiet calm of those at our publishers, Hardie Grant Books; particularly Jasmin Chua, Julie Pinkham and Martine Lleonart. I also love the work of Fran Berry, Keiran Rogers, Jenny Macmillan and website maestro, Greg 'Arv' Arvidsson, and acknowledge the contribution that they make to the success of the book. The absence of Clare Coney was duly noted.

Although Elaine Forrestal has been somewhat distracted by her hunt for a long-dead pirate, she has continued to be tolerant, supportive and loving. The formerly manic young beagle, Fling, is now a mature one-year-old: calm, sensible and affectionate.

Bargain hunter's survival guide

An introduction to buying great-value wines

INTRODUCTION

PETER FORRESTAL

Over the past year, there has been a great deal of corporate movement in the wine industry. Perhaps the biggest news has been the takeover of Southcorp by Beringer Blass (or Fosters) making one of the world's biggest wine companies. There will certainly be savings for Beringer Blass following consolidation. It remains to be seen if consumers will benefit. I guess we all feel a trifle concerned at so much power being focused in one group.

It's a bit like that in the retail sector as Coles and Woolworths continue their relentless march towards even greater domination. There have been encouraging signs that some of the independents are seeking a new role so that they can flourish. The Alliance of Independent Wine Merchants is working hard to offer their customers something different from the supermarket chains. Long may they flourish.

On the supermarket front, it appears that there will be significant moves to increase the amount of home brand products being offered by supermarkets. These have been very much part of the supermarket scene in Britain for many years and offer the supermarkets much better margins. While this can be seen to be making wine just another supermarket commodity, the widespread introduction of home brands may be irresistible. *Quaff* will keep you informed about the best of these wines.

It's been the year of films about wine with *Sideways* causing a stir – and, in the USA, boosting sales of pinot noir and choking interest in merlot. *Mondovino*, a documentary by James Nossiter, which looks at the globalisation of wine, has caused a fair bit of a stir around the world and will interest wine lovers.

In 2005, we've had a fantastic vintage almost everywhere in Australia and another record crop. Given the glut of red wine, we might not have needed that. The oversupply of wine has meant that some in the corporate world of wine have taken a battering. All companies report that it's a tough market and most have never found selling as hard. Of course, that is good news for consumers. There has probably never been a better time to be a winelover in Australia.

And what about us – we're back for a sixth year, and loving it. We reckon the thicker the wine jungle gets, the more consumers need guidance. It's so easy to find cheap wines – but harder than ever to know which are the good wines. Unless, of course, you have a copy of *Quaff* in your pocket.

Quaff online at is a great source of wine information and reviews, and the best way to keep your copy of *Quaff* up to date throughout the year. To receive weekly reviews of great-value wines, subscribe for FREE at www.quaff.com.au. We'll let you know as soon as the best new wines under $15 hit the market. Don't forget to tell your friends, and *Quaff* on!

ROLL OUT THE BARREL ... IT'S THE QUAFF AWARDS

The Quaff 2006 Awards

These are the stand-out wines from the *Quaff* tastings; they represent superlative quality and exceptional value for money.

**THE 2006 OBERON KANT MEMORIAL AWARD FOR THE QUINTESSENTIAL QUAFFER,
THE ULTIMATE AUSTRALIAN WINE UNDER $15** and
**THE QUAFF 2006 'Fillet Steak and Chips'
RED WINE OF THE YEAR AWARD**

2004 Zonte's Footstep Cabernet Malbec
How good is this! Zonte's Footstep is a relatively new label, which uses fruit from a 210-hectare vineyard in Langhorne Creek and involves marketer Zar Brooks, viticulturist Geoff Hardy, winemaker Ben Riggs, and vigneron John Pargeter. The 2003 vintage of Zonte's Footstep Cabernet Malbec was pleasant enough but lacked the vibrance and depth of flavour of this. Here is quintessential quaffing: rich, densely concentrated cassis, raspberry and red plum flavours, fleshy texture, ripe, fine tannins nicely balanced with refreshing acidity. Delicious. (See page 140.)

**THE QUAFF 2006 'Platinum Pillow'
CASK WINE OF THE YEAR**

De Bortoli Premium Reserve Merlot (2 litres)
The competition was hot this year – with four outstanding reds jousting for the 'Platinum Pillow'. I can't remember seeing such good-quality cask wines before: that glut is doing consumers of red casks a very big favour. The De Bortoli Merlot has lovely red berry aromas, is soft, round and full-bodied, smooth and pleasant in the mouth and has a nicely balanced finish. The fruit and the oak are in harmony, the tannins are restrained. If you are thinking about whooshability – and who isn't? – then this merlot has it by the bucket (or cask) full. (See page 21.)

THE QUAFF 2006 'Bubbly that Launched a Thousand Ships'
SPARKLING WINE OF THE YEAR

Sir James Pinot Noir Chardonnay

Sensationally good bubbly from Hardys master blender, Ed Carr. This has usually been a decent wine but I can't remember seeing the non-vintage Sir James looking this great before. It is fine, even delicate, has intense lemon citrus character with a hint of yeastiness, good weight, depth and length of flavour and neatly balanced acidity to finish. Terrific value. (See page 29.)

THE QUAFF 2006 'Baubles, Bubbles and Beads'
BEST SPARKLING WINE UNDER $10

Banrock Station Pinot Noir Chardonnay

For the second consecutive year this bright, vibrant bubbly remains unchallenged as the quality sparkling wine at the under $10 price point reinforcing – as if it needed reinforcing – the strength of Hardys sparkling wine portfolio. The Banrock Station sparkling white has bold acidity is lively with lemon citrus flavours and cool, refreshing acidity to finish. (See page 29.)

THE QUAFF 2006 'Whooshable'
WHITE WINE OF THE YEAR AWARD

2005 Jim Barry Watervale Riesling

From an outstanding vintage in the Clare Valley comes this brilliantly priced riesling. It is a very smart wine – and remarkably good value. The 2005 Jim Barry is beautifully floral, has intense lime and lemon juice flavours, wonderful zestiness and a long, dry, zingy finish. (See page 52.)

THE QUAFF 2006 'The Gluggable'
BEST WHITE WINE UNDER $10 AWARD

2004 Logan 'Apple Tree Flat' Chardonnay

From Central Ranges in New South Wales comes the Logan family's quaffing label and this impressive chardonnay: lean, tight and fine with intense white stone fruit and pink grapefruit flavours. A very modern style. (See page 44.)

THE QUAFF 2006 'Sausages and Chips'
BEST RED WINE UNDER $10 AWARD

2003 Beelgara 'Silky Oak' Shiraz

This is much more robust than most Riverina reds. You may need to decant this or give it a vigorous swirl before you taste – just to give it some air. It has plummy flavours, fleshy texture, reasonable integration of fruit and oak and firm, prominent tannins to finish. You'd forgive it for that especially if you served it with a hearty sirloin and a lusty, wine-based sauce. (See page 107.)

THE QUAFF 2006 'An Affair to Remember'
IMPORTED WHITE WINE OF THE YEAR AWARD

2003 Torres 'Vina Esmeralda', Spain

This is sourced from the mountainous area of the Upper Penedes using the heady aromatic varieties moscatel and gewürztraminer – as becomes immediately obvious when you open the bottle. This is wonderfully fragrant, has pristine grapey, muscaty flavours, and a gentle fruity finish that lingers. Serve chilled. Imported by the Spanish acquisition. (See page 163.)

THE QUAFF 2006 'Another Foreign Affair'
IMPORTED RED WINE OF THE YEAR AWARD

2004 La Belle Terrasse Shiraz, France

An impeccably clean, vibrant shiraz – from the Langedoc Roussillon in the South of France – that has juicy, even squishy raspberry and plum flavours before a nicely balanced finish. Imported by Southcorp. (See page 165.)

THE QUAFF 2006 'Any Port in a Storm'
FORTIFIED WINE OF THE YEAR AWARD

Morris Black Label Liqueur Muscat

A sensational Rutherglen muscat for less than $15! A terrific fortified by the master blender David Morris, which has typical grapey, raisiny character, is suprisingly rich and concentrated (for the price), has that irrestible lush, velvety texture and a gentle raisiny finish that lingers. (See page 155.)

THE QUAFF 2006 'For They Are Jolly Good Chaps'
WINERY OF THE YEAR AWARD

Queen Adelaide

What a great performance for a label that sells wines at the bargain basement price (between $7 and $8)! Queen Adelaide entered 13 wines in *Quaff* and had seven of these reviewed including Bloody Goods for the Riesling and the Cabernet Merlot and Good for the Cabernet Sauvignon. Sure Queen Adelaide is a brand based at Karadoc in the Murray Darling rather than a winery as such. Given the diversity of wineries, labels, brands, and multi-national conglomerates which contribute to *Quaff*, it seems reasonable to me to consider Queen Adelaide as a winemaking entity. And one thoroughly worth of the 2006 Winery of the Year title.

THE QUAFF 2006 'Move Over Darling'
BEST NEW LABEL AWARD

The Long Flat Wine Company

An auspicious debut for this label of Cheviot Bridge which releases varietal wines from classic vineyard regions at rock bottom prices. It entered four wines, three of which scored a Bloody Good rating: Yarra Valley Chardonnay, Adelaide Hills Sauvignon and Yarra Valley Pinot Noir.

HALL OF FAME: THE RELIABLES

After six years of sniffing and slurping through thousands of wines for *Quaff*, there are a few that have never failed to impress. The list is slowly reducing in size. However, those which remain have been recommended in every edition, regardless of vintage or label change, which is worth at least a polite round of applause:

Sparkling
Andrew Garrett Pinot Noir Chardonnay
Banrock Station Pinot Noir Chardonnay
Banrock Station Sparkling Shiraz
Omni

White
McWilliams Hanwood Chardonnay
Mitchelton 'Blackwood Park' Riesling
Moondah Brook Verdelho
Primo Estate 'La Biondina'
Rosemount Estate Semillon Chardonnay
Tahbilk Marsanne
Westend Estate 'Richland' Sauvignon Blanc

Red
Bleasdale Malbec
Peter Lehmann Shiraz Grenache
Rosemount Estate 'Diamond Label' Shiraz

Sweet and Fortified
Brown Brothers Spatlese Lexia
Penfolds Fortified Club
Penfolds Reserve Club Aged Tawny

You'll find these and a whole heap of other consistent performers listed in each chapter. Commit these names to memory, so that when you next find yourself in an unfamiliar bottleshop, you'll always be able to buy a good-value drink.

HOW THIS BOOK WORKS

So, what do we mean by good value?

Value means tasting – or drinking – a wine, enjoying it immensely, finding out the price and then saying to yourself: **'Bloody hell, does it really ONLY cost that much?'**

It's being happy to pay more for a wine than you actually paid. It's then – to a certain extent – gaining more enjoyment from that wine because you know you paid a reasonable price for it.

Value is relative, of course. There are plenty of $5 wines that are overpriced, just as there are $50 wines that provide just as much pleasure as wines three or four times the price. This is an important point: good value doesn't mean cheap. In recognition of this, a whole section of the book has been dedicated to wines over $15 – wines that I reckon offer exceptional value.

But I still believe – and anybody in the wine trade will agree – that **most wine bought in Australia for everyday consumption is still under $15 a bottle**. In fact, about 90 per cent of wine bought in Australia costs less than $15 a bottle. This is certainly where the dramatic discounting action is happening in the larger stores. And if you take into account that 50 per cent of all wines sales are casks, then the average price comes down to significantly less than $15 per 750 ml of wine.

So the majority of wines recommended in this book are still under $15.

How the wines were chosen

To start with, I approached all the major (and many smaller) wine companies in Australia, and asked them to submit samples of their under-$15 wines for tasting – as long as they would be available commercially from October 2005. Importers were asked to submit wines under $20. I was still receiving and tasting these wines right into August, which means that I was able to evaluate many, many 2005 vintage whites and 2004 reds (even a few 2005 reds) before they hit the retail shelves.

This means that *Quaff* contains more recommendations for wines you can actually go out and buy than any other wine guide.

The wines were all tasted blind – that is, I had no idea of the identity of the wine in the glass in front of me. In my view, this is the only fair way to assess wine: having even the slightest glimpse of the label, or a peek at a distinctive bottle shape, will influence the most determined taster. As always happens, I encountered some surprises: wines with big reputations that tasted very ordinary, and wines that I didn't expect to perform well coming up trumps on the tasting bench.

The list of great value wines over $15 was compiled from the extensive tastings I do as part of my everyday job as a wine writer. Those selected are the best value offerings of the last 12 months. They are recommended without the same level of guarantee that they'll definitely be commercially available at the time of publication – but I have tried to make sure you can still buy them.

A unique rating system

Some wines are better than others. So, within each chapter on the wines under $15, my selections have been grouped under three headings:

BLOODY GOOD – a delicious example of the style that over-delivers on quality and offers great value

GOOD – above-average example of the style that offers good value

PRETTY GOOD – if you're in the local drive-in bottleshop these are the reliable wines you can count on to provide a nice drink

So while I can recommend about 40 per cent of all the under-$15 wines I tried, I'd only rate about 10 per cent of them Bloody Good – and 60 per cent of the wines tasted I'd happily drive past in the bottleshop rather than drink again (a harsh but fair image).

I've tried to make tasting notes as informative, easy to read and evocative as possible. I've also tried to keep the often-confusing, technical wine language to a minimum base – but it does appear occasionally so there is a brief glossary on page 231 to help make sense of the jargon.

How much is it, and where can I get it?

These are possibly the two most important questions for a wine drinker. And only one of them is easy to answer.

How much is it? When I asked the wine companies to tell us how much their wine cost, they gave me a suggested retail price based on the wholesale price plus tax plus retailer mark-up. But the wine trade in Australia is a dynamic and fluctuating beast, with discounting, local retail patterns and various behind-the-scenes deals and promotions all leading to sometimes quite fluid pricing. So while I can offer the suggested retail price as a guide, you may find that the price on the shelf in your favourite store is different – it will hopefully be lower, but it may be higher.

You will also notice a few wines in the under-$15 chapters with a full suggested retail price of over $15; we've done this with wines that will be widely and regularly available for less on discount, and made it very clear how much you should be able to find each wine for if you shop around.

Where can you get it? Under-$15 wines tend to be produced in fairly large quantity, so we feel confident in saying that, unless otherwise stipulated, you should be able to find most of them at most bottleshops, fairly easily. Exceptions are self-explanatory: if a wine is only available through one retail chain or direct sales operation, for example, we have indicated that. But to help get you started on the road to discovery – and to finding the less widely available over-$15 wines – we have also included (starting on page 202) contact information for the distributors of all the wines, and listed recommended retailers in each state and territory.

Finally, all wines mentioned (apart from the casks, of course), are 750 ml bottles, unless otherwise specified.

VINTAGE REPORTS: 2005–2001

2005

Not only was the 2005 vintage another record one for the Australian wine industry (with 1.92 million tonnes harvested), but it was one of uniformly superb quality. In recent times any increase in the amount harvested has been due to vineyard expansion. In 2005, the increase was due to the ideal weather conditions – a long, mild growing season and perfectly timed rainfall – which resulted in disease-free fruit and higher yields. The exceptions were some parts of the Riverina and eastern Victoria, which were affected by heavy summer rains, and the southern areas of Western Australia, where the late ripening reds suffered because of April rains. Some regions felt that the quality was the best they'd seen in 30 years.

2004

With more than 1.8 million tonnes of grapes harvested, the 2004 vintage was Australia's largest ever – a whopping 25 per cent bigger than 2003's drought-affected crop. There were problems early and late in the season: some of the warmer regions such as the Barossa suffered heat stress (sunburned grapes) in February, and some of the cooler regions such as the Yarra Valley were caught with a few grapes still on the vine when heavy rains hit in April. But between these extremes, quality generally was good to very good. Yields were a little higher than average, too, which eases pressure on the supply of white wines, but only adds to the oversupply of reds.

2003

In some ways, a typical Australian vintage – warm and dry – but it was also unusually low-yielding. Indeed, it was the first time for many years that the crop levels were lower than the previous vintage, even with the first harvests from many new vineyards adding to the total. Quality across the board was good to very good, but there were fewer of the superlative wines found in 2002.

2002

Most of south-eastern Australia enjoyed an unusually cool summer, but while this resulted in some of the best grapes ever picked in the large inland regions and warmer premium regions such as the Barossa, the further south in the country you go, the more difficult those cool conditions proved in terms of ripening the grapes. So while 2002 cheap reds often showed the effects of the good vintage – great dark colour, heaps of flavour – and the aromatic whites and chardonnays we've tasted were certainly unusually flavoursome, you need to be a little choosier buying more expensive wines from the trendier, premium, cooler-climate regions.

2001

If 2002 was characterised by its cool growing season, 2001 was the opposite: some of the hottest weather on record had two effects on the grape crop. One was a reduction in yield, meaning some very concentrated flavours in the wines – particularly reds – and the other was a less-than-brilliant year for white wines, especially aromatics. Sure, some good white wines were made, but they don't have the same zesty aromatic quality as the 2002s.

Cheap and cheerful

Cask wines worth buying

THE BEST CASK WINES AROUND

As ever, the state of cask wines reflects what is happening in the wider wine industry itself. The vast vineyard plantings of the past five to ten years and the more gradual expansion of our export markets has meant that there is a glut of grapes. As was the case last year, the glut is mainly in red wine production. This has had an amazing impact on the quality of the best red casks. I've not seen better red cask wines than those recommended as Bloody Good in this year's *Quaff*. I have complained that too many reds in cask have too much chippy oak and too much added tannin making them unbalanced and leaving the consumer with a powerful grippy and bitter aftertaste. While that is still the case with plenty of the cask reds on the market, it is certainly not true of the best.

There's been some improvement in the quality of white casks since last year as supply has been better able to meet demand for white grapes. Some people complain that cask whites are too sweet. If you are looking for drier styles, those labelled chardonnay are your best bet.

The loud cry 'smaller is better' continues to echo through the cask market as 21 out of the 28 recommended casks were 2 litre. Five years ago, in the first edition of *Quaff*, the standard size was 4 litre and smaller casks were very much the exception.

All the casks are non-vintage, unless otherwise specified.

The reliables –
consistent-quality wines, year in, year out

Yalumba are once again the most consistent producer of cask wines – as they have been for all six editions of *Quaff*. Hardys and Banrock Station are also very impressive and have been represented each year in this book.

Buying and Drinking Casks – Some Tips

Best before

Look for the 'use by' date on the cask before you buy. The wine will be at its freshest in the first three to six months or so after it is bottled and begin to get stale at about nine months.

All things must pass

The reason that we prefer smaller casks to larger ones is that once the cask is opened it begins the slow process of oxidation and will eventually lose its freshness and lively fruitiness. The cask will be at its best for a week or so after opening.

What am I drinking?

One of the big changes in cask wines in the past six years has been the move away from 'Fruity Dry White' or 'Classic Dry Red' to varietal names – Semillon Trebbiano Chardonnay or Shiraz Cabernet. In the former case, you have no idea of the grape varieties used in the blend – and it's most likely to include some cheap (read inferior) varieties. When the grapes are spelt out on the label you know exactly what you are getting – and the wines are likely to be better.

White Casks

⬤► BLOODY GOOD

Yalumba Reserve Selection Chardonnay (2 litre) $13.95

There's little doubt that Yalumba makes a great deal of effort with their 2-litre casks – and this, the top white cask, clearly illustrates that. At a time when there is a bit of a strain on supplies of chardonnay, Yalumba have maintained or improved the quality of this cask. It's a good drink: soft, round, impeccably clean, less oaky than most, has attractive viscous texture, good weight, lively ripe peachy flavours and a reasonably dry finish that lingers.

Yalumba Reserve Selection Sauvignon Blanc Semillon (2 litre) $13.95

For the last four years, the Yalumba 2-litre Sauvignon Blanc has either been the best or one of the best cask whites in our line-up. Because of the surge in popularity of semillon sauvignon blanc blends, Yalumba have decided to use their sauvignon to flesh out that blend and drop the sauvignon blanc casks. I thought this might have been a problem until this Sauvignon Blanc Semillon showed up as one of the top wines in this year's cask tasting. Ripe tropical flavours, lively mouthfeel, some mid-palate sweetness and a reasonably dry finish.

⬤► GOOD

Kaiser Stuhl Crisp Dry White (5 litre) $13.95

While not particularly dry, this has attractive flora aromas, some grapey flavours, is fresh and clean with a pleasant sweetish aftertaste.

Lindemans 'Cawarra' Chardonnay (2 litre) $12.95

This has chippy oak aromas but is much better on the palate where the oak does not dominate the fruit. It's clean, fresh and quite dry to finish.

Yalumba Spatlese Fruity White (2 litre) $11.95

If you like some sweetness in your cask whites, then this is the one for you. It's fragrant with some grapey aromas, is light-bodied, pleasantly sweet and has some lively crispness to clean up the finish.

▸ PRETTY GOOD

Banrock Station White Shiraz (2 litre) $13.50

This lightly tinged pink cask wine is less sweet than many of its competitors and so will appeal to some. Soft and clean with some light redcurrant flavours.

Brown Brothers Fruity White (10 litre) $55

The size of this cask, unique to Brown Brothers, appeals to some just because of its size. This wine is clean, fresh, lively, fruity and quite sweet.

Coolabah Fresh Dry White (4 litre) $11.95

There's plenty of grapey fruit character in this cask wine: it's fresh, clean and lively with a pleasant mouthfeel.

De Bortoli Premium Semillon Trebbiano Chardonnay (4 litre) $17.95

A soft, round, fruity wine with some chippy oak notes and a dry, grippy finish.

Lindemans Premium Varietal Chardonnay (4 litre) $18.95

This is noticeably drier than many cask whites and has a charry oak character on the nose – though this is less evident on the palate. It's soft and round and easy-drinking with a pleasing oaky grip on the finish.

Queen Adelaide Chardonnay [2 litre] $12.95

I noted during the blind tasting that this doesn't have the obvious oak of, for example, the Lindemans Chardonnay. In fact, the style of the Queen Adelaide has, for some time, been unwooded. It is clean, fresh and softer than many yet is still quite dry – so there's a slight grip to finish.

2004 Yalumba Colombard Chardonnay [2 litre] $11.95

While this is a little bland, it is fresh, crisp and quite dry: a pleasant drink. One of very few white casks labelled by vintage.

Red Casks

 BLOODY GOOD

⭐ De Bortoli Premium Reserve Merlot (2 litre) $12.95

**THE QUAFF 2006 'PLATINUM PILLOW'
CASK WINE OF THE YEAR**

The competition was hot this year – with four outstanding reds jousting for the 'Platinum Pillow'. I can't remember seeing such good-quality cask wines before: that glut is doing consumers of red casks a very big favour. The De Bortoli Merlot has lovely red berry aromas, is soft, round and full-bodied, smooth and pleasant in the mouth and has a nicely balanced finish. The fruit and the oak are in harmony, the tannins are restrained. If you are thinking about whooshability – and who isn't? – then this merlot has it by the bucket (or cask) full.

De Bortoli Premium Reserve Shiraz (2 litre) $12.95

A delightful red with attractive red berry flavours – some dark plums, perhaps mulberries, red cherries – quite rich and concentrated, smooth, almost fleshy. A good drink at a great price.

Hardys Shiraz (3 litre) $21

The performance of the top three shiraz casks in this year's *Quaff* tastings emphasises why this variety has become the workhorse of the Australian industry. The Hardys casks (including Banrock Station) have performed extremely well especially in the past two years. This has attractive red berry flavours, is smooth and gulpable, and has excellent balance between the fruit and oak and between the fruit and tannins.

Yalumba Reserve Selection Shiraz (2 litre) $13.95

I couldn't believe my luck. The red cask tasting is pretty hard work and I'd come to the last bracket – as they say 'it was the last quarter and we were kicking with the wind' – when I came across four remarkably good cask wines. No excessive chippy oak, no harsh tannins. The Yalumba Shiraz has pleasant red berry aromas, red plum characters, good richness and more concentration of flavour than you'd expect in a cask wine. And the balance on the finish made it very good drinking. Just what you want.

 GOOD

Banrock Station Shiraz Cabernet Sauvignon (2 litre) $13.50

This is just a shade less impressive than the top reds. It is less oaky and less tannic than most red casks, is lively and well-balanced with ripe plum and redcurrant flavours. A good drink.

Lindemans 'Cawarra' Cabernet Merlot (2 litre) $12.95

Both 'Cawarra' casks looked good to me. The red is clean with fresh red berry flavours, gentle oak and restrained tannin.

PRETTY GOOD

Banrock Station Cabernet Merlot (2 litre) $13.50

Not as rich or concentrated as the other Banrock red but pleasant, supple, a smooth pleasing mouthfeel and a dry finish. Restrained use of oak and tannins.

Brown Brothers Dry Red (10 litre) $55

Could do with more concentration of fruit but will appeal to followers of the Brown Brothers stable. It's reasonably oaky but not over the top.

Yalumba Classic Dry Red (2 litre) $11.95
> This has some red berry flavours, a chewy texture and firm finish.

Yalumba Reserve Selection Cabernet Sauvignon (2 litre) $13.95
> This is clean and well made with quite powerful flavours; a bit oaky and firm on the finish.

Yalumba Reserve Selection Cabernet Shiraz (2 litre) $13.95
> Quite a powerfully flavoured red with heaps of tannins on the finish, which are in reasonable balance with the fruit.

Fortified Casks

▶ BLOODY GOOD

Penfolds 'Wood Aged' Port (2 litre) $11.95

Clearly the best of the cask fortifieds available at present. The Penfolds Club, which was the star last year, still has great flavour but is spoilt by very strong spirit on the finish. This is soft, round and silky with pleasant toffee and treacle flavours and a gentle, fine finish.

▶ GOOD

Seppelt Medium Dry Sherry (2 litre) $15.95

There is an oxidative character that you get with sherry that is apparent on the nose of this fortified. It is soft, round and silky, semi-sweet, yet with a mouth-puckering dryish finish.

Seppelt 'Solero' Cream Sherry (2 litre) $15.95

Southcorp do have this sector of the fortified all trussed up. This cream sherry has attractive flor yeast on the nose, a soft, sweet palate and a lively seductive finish. True to the cream sherry style.

▶ PRETTY GOOD

Angoves 'Paddle Wheel' Muscat (2 litre flagon) $9.10

This flagon is fragrant with those distinctive grapey aromas of muscat. It is soft, round, rich and sweet with raisin and treacle flavours.

Penfolds 'Wood Aged' Muscat (2 litre) $11.95

This is a bit short on the delicious raisiny flavours of bottled muscat but is soft, round and viscous with a treacle-like texture and a slightly tangy grip to finish.

More than froth and bubble

Sparkling wines under $15

SPARKLING WINES UNDER $15

It's hard to believe the consistency of Ed Carr and the team from Hardys. Once again, as they have in each of the six editions of *Quaff*, the Banrock Station bubblies have been rated Bloody Good. The Pinot Noir Chardonnay is Best Sparkling under $10 for the second year in a row and the Banrock Station Reserve Sparkling Shiraz – last year's Wine of the Year – wins the Sparkling Red category once more. Better still for Hardys, Best Sparkling Wine stays within the portfolio as it is won by the best Sir James Pinot Noir Chardonnay I've seen.

There are a few welcome intruders – Four Sisters, Roberts Estate and Bimbadgen – but sparkling wine at this price point is the domain of the large companies. It's a remarkable feat that huge companies – such as Southcorp (Seppelt, Seaview, Lindemans), Orlando (Jacobs Creek, Richmond Grove, Wyndham), Beringer Blass (Wolf Blass, Yellowglen, Andrew Garrett) and Hardys – and the modestly large Yalumba, McWilliams and De Bortoli are able to make vast quantities of good quality bubbly while maintaining consistency of style from year to year. Amazingly, more than half those reviewed have a recommended retail price of $10 or less – in keeping with the trend in other editions of *Quaff*.

All sparkling wines are non-vintage, unless otherwise indicated.

The reliables –
consistent-quality wines, year in, year out

The following producers of fizz make regular appearances in *Quaff* – and so you can buy their wines with confidence: Banrock Station, Sir James and Omni; Seaview and Seppelt; Andrew Garrett and Wolf Blass 'Eaglehawk'; Jacobs Creek and Carrington; De Bortoli and McWilliams 'Hanwood'. The Brown Brothers Moscato – our 2002 Wine of the Year – has appeared in five of the six editions of *Quaff* and gets the Bloody Good rating for the second year in a row.

Buying and Drinking Bubbly – Some Tips

Pity about the marketing

I've been delighted with the disappearance of the term 'champagne', which was in the past used to describe Aussie bubblies. It's also been good to see that most producers are describing their wines by the grape varieties in the blend (hence Pinot Noir Chardonnay). More difficult to believe is the practice of adding some French words to the names of Australian sparkling wines – apparently to impress the consumer. In my view, words like *brut* (which means 'dry') and *cuvée* ('a blend') are meaningless in this context.

Look for places with a quick turnover

I noticed that the tougher conditions in retail land have slowed down the sales of bubblies, so much so that a higher proportion of sparkling wines than usual appeared tired and past their best. The most impressive wines had clean, fresh, lively, up-front flavours. As these wines don't improve with cellaring, buy from shops that have a quick turnover of stock.

Drink cold

These budget-priced quaffers are best served nicely chilled to enhance their fresh, lively character and zingy acidity. Enjoy. *Quaff* on!

Corked?

With the wide-scale acceptance of screwcap closures on whites and plenty of reds, the incidence of corked wines in the *Quaff* tastings has been reduced. As very few sparkling wine producers have gone to crown seal (Domaine Chandon and Seppelt Great Western are exceptions), I've noticed a significant number of corked wines in the sparkling wine tastings. Swirl, sniff and check that there are no strange off characters before you drink your bubblies. Look for any mouldy, wet-hessian, wet-dog aromas: anything that doesn't seem quite right.

White Sparkling

📍 **BLOODY GOOD**

⭐ **Banrock Station Pinot Noir Chardonnay** $7.95
> THE QUAFF 2006 'Baubles, Bubbles and Beads'
> BEST SPARKLING WINE UNDER $10
> For the second consecutive year this bright, vibrant bubbly remains unchallenged as the quality sparkling wine at the under $10 price point: reinforcing – as if it needed to be articulated – the strength of Hardys sparkling wine portfolio. The Banrock Station sparkling white is bold and lively with lemon citrus flavours and cool, refreshing acidity.

⭐ **Sir James Pinot Noir Chardonnay** $12
> THE QUAFF 2006 'Bubbly that Launched a Thousand Ships'
> SPARKLING WINE OF THE YEAR
> Sensationally good bubbly from Hardys master blender, Ed Carr. This has usually been a decent wine but I can't remember seeing the non-vintage Sir James looking this great before. It is fine, even delicate, has intense lemon citrus character with a hint of yeastiness, good weight, depth and length of flavour and neatly balanced acidity to finish. Terrific value.

Yellowglen 'Yellow' $12
> A neatly crafted bubbly in which the flavour builds as you drink. Attractive creamy texture, bright lemony acidity on a lingering finish.

GOOD

Andrew Garrett Pinot Noir Chardonnay $14.95

This is an interesting bubbly that showed up in tastings much the same as it did last year. Then, Max loved it for its bready, yeasty, apply smells and crisp, fine finish and I thought it was OK. This year I felt it was bold, yeasty and a bit over the top. Some of the tasting panel agreed. Others, however, took a similar view to that which Max expressed last year and were strong supporters, enjoying its straw-like aromas, power and length. It's one of the reliables – appearing in every edition of *Quaff*.

Bimbadgen Ridge Sparkling Semillon $12.50

And now for something completely different: a sparkling semillon from Bimbadgen in the Hunter Valley. And it's delicious: fresh and vibrant, with lemon citrus flavours. Clean and crisp.

1999 Lindemans Reserve Pinot Noir Chardonnay Pinot Meunier $14.95

This has been given the deluxe treatment of the three classic Champagne grapes, chardonnay from the Adelaide Hills and pinot from Coonawarra, plus 24 months bottle maturation. It's very easy to drink: soft, round, creamy with lemon citrus flavours and a hint of toastiness.

Omni $9.95

Need I say it – this is another sparkling wine from the Hardys portfolio. Oh boy. And the quality is good – and it's cheap. Restrained on the nose, positive lemon citrus flavours, refreshing gentle acidity.

Seaview Grande Cuvee $8.95

> The blend is predominantly pinot noir with muscatel, chenin and semillon sourced from different regions of South Australia. It has attractive yeasty fragrances, lemon sherbet flavours and racy acidity before its sweetness produces a gentle finish.

Seppelt Great Western Brut Reserve $7.95

> More than enough old favourites performed up to expectation in this year's tastings to suggest that the grand old Australian wine industry (or should that be the bright, new, technologically-clever Australian wine industry) is still able to provide excellent value at all price points. The cheap Seppelt and Seaview bubblies – all made at Southcorp's Great Western huge sparkling wine facility – performed very well indeed. This was my favourite with its attractive mouthfeel, yeasty characters on the mid-palate and gentle lemony acidity on a pleasant finish. Value.

Seppelt Great Western Imperial Reserve $7.95

> While pleasant and straightforward, the Imperial Reserve is lifted by its attractive mouthfeel, crisp lively bubbles and fine lingering finish.

🍾 PRETTY GOOD

Andrew Garrett 'Garrett' Brut $11

> Lemony, yeasty characters, creamy texture, lively acidity to finish.

Angas Brut $7.95

> Some yeastiness on the nose, oomph on the palate, pleasant, gentle, dryish finish.

Carrington Brut Reserve $6.95

> Clean, fresh and very lively, steely structure and strong acidity.

2004 Cleanskin Reserve RP04 Sparkling Pinot Noir Chardonnay $9.95
A touch developed on the nose but soft, fine and creamy on the palate with lemon citrus flavours. From the Woolworths stable.

Four Sisters Pinot Noir Chardonnay $14.90
The first bubbly for this popular Victorian quaffing label: candied aromas, pleasant mouthfeel, strong acidity relieved by sweetness on the finish.

Jacobs Creek Brut Cuvee Chardonnay Pinot Noir $10.95
Some attractive yeastiness, soft almost creamy texture, gentle fine finish.

Jean Pierre & Co. Celebration Brut $5.65
Fragrant, bright, fairy-floss flavours, creamy texture, sweet to finish with some lively acidity. Cheap and fair value.

McWilliams 'Hanwood' Pinot Noir Chardonnay $12
Lightly flavoured with some pleasant straw characters and soft, round and creamy texture. Easy to drink.

Seaview Brut de Brut $8
This is soft, straightforward and easy-drinking with strong acidity.

Wolf Blass 'Eaglehawk' Cuvee Brut $10
Lively with intense lemon citrus flavours and a pretty firm finish.

Red Sparkling

BLOODY GOOD

Banrock Station 'The Reserve' Sparkling Shiraz $12.95

Last year's batch of this wine was the *Quaff* Wine of the Year; this year's is unquestionably in the same league – you will not find a better sparkling shiraz for less than $15. If you want to pay more than $15 a bottle you might find one that is better than this – you won't find many – and you'll need to starting looking at spending more than $25. This wine is a bargain – and the quintessential quaffer: bold, rich, ripe, deep brambly, plummy flavours, velvety texture, and a fine, lively finish. *Quaff* on!

Sir James Sparkling Pinot Noir Shiraz $12

Australian sparkling red is a moveable feast. Some people insist that the classic Seppelt interpretation – no obvious oak flavour, soft and spicy shiraz fruit – is the only true way, while others are more adventurous, accepting big, chunky, new-oak matured sparkling cabernet. Personally, while I lean towards the classic, I'm mostly concerned about personality and deliciousness: if the foaming purple liquid in my glass has a smell that makes me want to drink it, and if it delivers complexity, satisfying depth and sheer joyfulness in the mouth, then I'm happy. And this new wine from Hardys does just that: it smells enticing, leafy, spicy, herbal, even flowery (thanks to the pinot), and is sweet, juicy, silky and spicy in the mouth. Quail marinated in szechuan pepper and chilli and grilled over charcoal, please.

GOOD

De Bortoli 'Emeri' Sparkling Durif $10.50

Reviewed in *Quaff* for the third year in a row, this shows just how well the robust red grape durif does in the Riverina and also how well it can do in sparkling reds. While it was thought to be a bit feral last year, the present batch should have much more universal appeal. Powerful, ripe red berry flavours, creamy texture, good weight, lively acidity.

Omni Red $9.95

A straightforward but appealing sparkling red – from Hardys – with concentrated plum and blackberry flavours, some sweetness and refreshing acidity to finish.

Tyrrells Sparkling Cabernet Sauvignon $13.95

A surprise packet for me: rich, powerful, earthy, even leathery – this is a robust sparkling red with dense red berry fruit, good weight and substantial tannins. It's lively and approachable.

 **PRETTY GOOD**

Andrew Garrett Sparkling Burgundy $14.95

I'm staggered that Beringer Blass would use the old-fashioned – and soon to be outlawed – term to describe this sparkling red. It's the only example that I'm aware of still on the market. Needed a good swirl to bring out its best, though smooth, rich and concentrated on the palate with powerful acidity to finish.

Pink Bubbles

 GOOD

De Bortoli 'Windy Peak' Pinot Noir Chardonnay $12.50
From De Bortoli's Victorian range comes a very good bubbly: delicate pink tinge (what the wine buffs used to call 'partridge eye'), hint of raspberry, lively flavours, creamy texture, crisp zingy finish. For the fun times!

Minchinbury Fine Private Cuvee $7
This is quite intense with clear strawberry flavours, a clean, lively palate and an attractive gentle finish.

Omni Pink $9.95
A clean, fresh, pleasant, lightly pink bubbly with gentle strawberry flavours, a fine almost delicate mousse, and a gentle, soft finish.

PRETTY GOOD

Carrington Blush $6.95
A well-made sparkling rosé that has bright honeysuckle and strawberry flavours and a clear, fresh finish.

Hardys Regional Reserve Classic Cuvee Pink $6.95
A fragrant, light pink sparkler with gentle bubbles and some sweetness.

Sweet Sparkling

🍾 BLOODY GOOD

2004 Brown Brothers Moscato $14

The 2002 *Quaff* Wine of the Year was the 2001 Brown Brothers Moscato and this is the best since. As well as having a superb fragrant bouquet – all those grapey, honeysuckle, rose petal aromas – it has a refreshing natural acidity to prevent the sweetness from becoming cloying. Just delicious. *Quaff* on!

2005 Two Hands 'Brilliant Disguise' Moscato $13.50

No disguises here – just brilliance: everything is absolutely spot-on with this wonderfully refreshing, foaming grapey fruit bomb. Modelled on the gorgeous, sherbety, fizzy wines made from the moscato grape in Italy's north-east, this is musky, perfumed Barossa Valley frontignac (like moscato, also a member of the muscat family of grapes), bottled halfway through fermentation at just 6.5 per cent alcohol, retaining a dollop of natural grape sugar and some of the gentle gas from ferment. But it's not just the joyful, sherbety style that's perfect – the chunky 500 ml bottle also feels lovely in the palm, looks lovely in the fridge (especially lined up in a row in the fridge door), and is exceptionally well-priced at $13.50 a throw. I know what I'll be drinking a lot of this summer. Bravo to all the hands.

🍾 GOOD

Omni Blue $9.95

Acidity is the key here. It's fragrant with alluring muscaty, grapey aromas and is sweet and full-flavoured. All this puts into balance the crisp, clean acidity that refreshes the palate and prevents the wine from becoming cloying.

▰▶ PRETTY GOOD

2004 Chateau Tanunda 'Barossa Tower' Moscato $14.95

A gently aromatic sweetie from the Barossa that is very easy to drink.

2004 Gapsted 'Victorian Alps' Moscato $14.95

This is very sweet but has character as well as freshness and good grapey flavours.

Nova 'Tickled Pink' Rosé $9.95

A non-vintage, slightly sparkling sweetie – described as the light, spritz red which it is – from the Riverina's Westend and enjoyed by me and the serious panel that I taste with, almost in spite of ourselves. There is a light onion skin colour, a gentle fizz, some obvious grapey flavour of muscat, and an icing sugar sweetness. Gentle, soft and appealing.

2005 Trentham Estate 'La Famiglia' Moscato $12.50

Attractive floral aromas, luscious sweet texture and fresh grapey flavours that linger.

Bottled sunshine

White wines under $15

CHARDONNAY

Those who predicted the demise of chardonnay a few years ago crying, 'Anything but chardonnay', could not have got it more wrong. The amount of chardonnay crushed in Australia in 2005 was 416,000 tonnes – up 34 per cent on the previous vintage and almost double the crush five years ago when the first edition of *Quaff* appeared. Interestingly, at that time, there was more of the bland workhorse grape variety sultana produced (250,000 tonnes) than chardonnay. As the Australian wine industry insists on better, more classic varieties, decreasing demand for sultana has seen thousands of hectares pulled out and its crush drop to about a quarter of its volume five years ago.

So Australian chardonnay is more popular than ever before. What I love about it is the attractive ripe fruit sweetness that gives the best examples a gentle softness on the mid-palate, a delightful mouthfeel.

Chardonnays that sell at $10 or below need to be sourced, wholly or in large part, from the warm to hot irrigated areas along the Murray in South Australia, Victoria or New South Wales. The best tend to be delicious, straightforward whites, which rely on ripe fruit flavours for their easy drinkability. With careful viticulture and meticulous wine-making, it is possible to produce some of these wines in huge volumes without risking quality or consistency.

Chardonnays that sell for between $10 and $15 tend to be sourced, at least in part, from premium wine regions and from lower yielding vineyards. With more concentrated fruit, it is possible to use winemaking techniques that will produce more complex and therefore more interesting wines. These will be more full-bodied, have more weight, more richness, greater concentration and power.

The reliables –
consistent-quality wines, year in, year out

Regular recommendations over the last six editions of *Quaff* include McWilliams 'Hanwood' and Yalumba 'Oxford Landing'.

Buying and Drinking Chardonnay – Some Tips

Personal preferences

Not every wine recommended in *Quaff* will appeal to everyone. In this chapter, there are some wines in which oak flavours dominate. Some people love these while others find them undrinkable. The descriptions of the wines always take this into account, so that you are not surprised (except pleasantly) after you've bought a wine.

When to drink

Although some more expensive chardonnays benefit from a few years bottle age, at this price point they are often better when reasonably young. Unwooded chardonnay, therefore, is best drunk within a year of vintage. Those that have seen some oak are sometimes better between 12 and 24 months of age than they are at a younger age – when the oak will have become better integrated with the fruit. Most wines in this chapter are from the 2004 vintage with a couple from 2003 and some from 2005. This is pretty much on a par with other editions of *Quaff*.

Unwooded Chardonnay

▶ BLOODY GOOD

2004 Browns of Padthaway Unwooded Chardonnay $16

The Brown family are the largest independent grape grower in the region and are making increasing volumes under their own label. This gem shows just how good Padthaway can be as a region for producing chardonnay: vibrant and fresh with delicious pure fruit – ripe, peachy, melony and tropical.

2004 Elderton Unwooded Chardonnay $13.95

Who says the Barossa can't make terrific chardonnay! While this did need a bit of a vigorous swirl to clean up the nose, the palate is fresh and lively with cool white peach and nectarine flavours, reasonable weight and a gentle finish.

▶ GOOD

2004 Evans & Tate 'Gnangara' Unwooded Chardonnay $13.50

It's 30 years since Evans & Tate first produced a wine under the Gnangara label. This has rich, ripe peachy fruit, an attractive mouthfeel, surprising concentration for the style, and a soft, clean, refreshing finish.

2004 Xabregas Unwooded Chardonnay $13.95

Xabregas owns three large vineyards in Mount Barker and the major stake in the Porongurup winery, so it has Di Miller make some wines under its own label. Most of these sell for less than $15. This has ripe tropical fruit and a lively palate with strongish acidity to finish.

2005 Yalumba 'Y Series' Unwooded Chardonnay $11.95

> The Yalumba white wine portfolio is particularly strong: this is a fresh, lively white with lemon citrus and tropical fruit flavours, a pleasant mouthfeel and zingy cleansing finish.

◀ PRETTY GOOD

2005 Angoves 'Stonegate' $7.95

> Delicate tropical fruit flavours, clean and easy-drinking, touch of sweetness.

2005 Capel Vale CV Unwooded Chardonnay $14.95

> Bright, ripe tropical fruit flavours, uncomplicated but lively.

2004 Morambro Creek Unwooded Chardonnay $14.95

> Small producer from Padthaway making some good wines. This is rich and concentrated with ripe tropical flavours and a clean, lively finish.

2004 Taylors 'Promised Land' Unwooded Chardonnay $13

> Needs a good swirl to start but fresh, lively and fruity.

2004 Tobacco Road Unwooded Chardonnay $11

> A new label from the Victorian Alps, presents a gently flavoursome white with ripe tropical fruit flavours.

2005 Upper Reach Unwooded Chardonnay $14.95

> Attractive Swan Valley white that has gentle, ripe flavours. Mainly cellar door.

2005 Zilzie Unwooded Chardonnay $14.95

> All the promise of 2005 – delicate lemon citrus flavours, good weight and concentration.

Chardonnay

 BLOODY GOOD

⭐ **2004 Logan 'Apple Tree Flat' Chardonnay** $9.95
THE QUAFF 2006 'The Gluggable'
BEST WHITE WINE OF THE YEAR UNDER $10 AWARD
From Central Ranges in New South Wales comes the Logan
family's quaffing label and this impressive chardonnay:
lean, tight and fine with intense white stone fruit and pink
grapefruit flavours. A very modern style.

2004 Long Flat Wine Company Chardonnay $13.95
Cheviot Bridge has been making some terrific wines in the
past few years including some impressive wines under this
label. Although they distinguish between their Long Flat
range of multi-regional wines and the Long Flat Wine Co
regional varietals (see www.cheviotbridge.com.au), I find
the similarity of the names a source of confusion and the
Wine Co name a mouthful. Still, this Yarra Valley chardonnay is a beauty: a huge burst of flavour, profusely fragrant,
zesty.

2005 Sandalford 'Element' Chardonnay $12.95
Another example that proves the resurgence at
Sandalford is not confined to the premium wines. This is
the best 'Element' Chardonnay that I've seen yet: soft,
round, easy-drinking with lemon citrus and honeydew
melon flavours, which finishes with ripe tropical fruits
that linger. Delicate oak.

2003 Simon Gilbert Card Collection Chardonnay $15

The Card Collection of wines from New South Wales wine-maker Simon Gilbert features a series of colourful 19th century educational cards that have been passed down through the Gilbert family (one of Simon's ancestors, Joseph Gilbert, owned the original Pewsey Vale vineyard in the Eden Valley in the latter half of the 1800s). In most cases, I've found the wines inside the bottles don't quite live up to the quality of the package – but this chardonnay, made from grapes sourced from the Central Ranges of New South Wales, is an exception: it's really aromatic, tangy, complex and rich, with heaps of flavour and a mineral-like dry finish that you don't expect to find in chardy at this price.

 GOOD

2004 Angoves 'Bear Crossing' Chardonnay $8.95

A regular favourite of *Quaff* delivering straightforward but decent ripe melony flavours and a juicy mouthfeel. Factor in the price and you have a good-value quaffer.

2004 De Bortoli 'Deen Vat 7' Chardonnay $9.95

Light-bodied chardonnay with gentle cedary oak, some intensity of flavour, good weight and concentration. Fine, and impressive for the price.

2005 Hamiltons Ewell 'Sturt River' Chardonnay $14

Ripe, intense, sweet fruit flavours with a whiff of confec-tionary, pleasing mouthfeel and fresh, slightly sweet finish.

2004 Houghton Chardonnay $11.95

There is nothing like an old reliable to stir the heart. I love them, especially when renewing the acquaintance in a blind tasting. The winemaking team at Houghton have access to huge quantities of quality Western Australian fruit and so they are able to consistently deliver tremendous value for money. Houghton's chief winemaker, Rob Bowen, was delighted with the 2004 vintage because of its atypical settled warm weather until the grapes were harvested statewide. Wines like this bear out his assessment: it's fresh, clean and lively, has attractive ripe tropical sweet fruit of good intensity and a satisfying fruity finish.

2003 Kirrihill Estates 'Companions' Chardonnay $12.95

A good quaffer from this large Clare Valley producer: a fine, nicely balanced white, which is ripe with fresh melony flavours, cedary oak and a gentle, easy finish.

2004 Little Penguin Chardonnay $10.95

Developed by Southcorp to fight Yellowtail for market share on the US market, this Little Penguin is light-bodied, juicy and lively with ripe peachy, tropical fruit flavours. Good value.

2004 Peter Lehmann Chardonnay $14.95

This is a fruit-driven chardonnay showing peach and lemon citrus flavours, soft in the mid-palate with powerfully crisp acidity to finish.

2004 Cookoothama Chardonnay $14.95

This chardonnay will appeal to many for its power, weight, richness and concentration of cedary oak flavours. For oak lovers mainly.

2004 Sticks Chardonnay $14.95

A Yarra Valley chardonnay from one of the long-term residents, Rob 'Sticks' Dolan. It is delightfully floral, round and soft with sweet peachy fruit and gentle refreshing acidity.

2004 Terra Felix Chardonnay $14.95

The chardonnay for this second label of Central Victoria's Tallarook is very pleasing: clean, fresh, lemon citrus and cedary oak flavours, creamy texture and crisp, lively finish.

2004 Trentham Estate Chardonnay $14.50

Surprisingly fine for a chardonnay from Mildura but Tony Murphy and the team at Trentham are past masters at surprise: this has intense white stone fruit (nectarines, white peach) flavours, a pleasant smooth and viscous mouthfeel and a gentle lingering finish. The 2005 lacked the charm of the previous vintage with very dominant oak.

2004 Wolf Blass 'Yellow Label' Chardonnay $13

You'll know it's a Wolf Blass wine by the dominating toasty oak. Still, there are ripe peachy flavours, some vitality and heaps of character. Mainly for the oak lovers.

2004 Zilzie Chardonnay $14.95

For my money, this is worth the extra few dollars more than the Zilzie second-string 'Buloke Reserve', though it may need a bit of a swirl when you open the bottle. There's plenty of flavour – cedary oak and ripe melon – and the temptation to whoosh it down.

◼▶ PRETTY GOOD

2004 Andrew Garrett Chardonnay $14

A good commercial chardonnay from Beringer Blass' huge winery at Nuriootpa – it has a light body and ripe melon flavours.

2004 Barwick Estates 'St Johns Brook' Chardonnay $13.95

One of the better wines from this large company with young vineyards in Pemberton, the Blackwood Valley and Margaret River. It is clean and fresh, has some tropical flavours and a soft finish.

2004 Bleasdale Chardonnay $13.50

From Langhorne Creek's oldest winery comes a light-bodied chardonnay with some concentration of peach and melon flavours and a gentle, soft finish.

2004 Buller 'Caspia' Chardonnay $10

From the 'Murray's green banks' and Rutherglen's Buller family comes this cheap, straightforward chardonnay, which is clean and fresh.

2004 Dal Broi 'Yarranvale Station' Chardonnay $10.95

This is easy-drinking from the Riverina: soft, creamy texture, light cedary oak and peachy flavours.

2004 Gapsted Chardonnay $14.95

A pleasant chardonnay from the Victorian Alps that is tightly framed, feels good in the mouth and has gentle cool flavours.

2005 McPherson Chardonnay $9

This is perfectly acceptable quaffing wine – fresh and lively with slightly confected, bubblegum characters.

2004 McWilliams 'Hanwood' Chardonnay $12

The most consistent Aussie chardonnay with appearances in each of the six editions of *Quaff*. Showing some peachy, melony flavours and a touch of finesse.

2004 Penfolds 'Rawsons Retreat' $9.95

There's heaps of ripe flavour in this entry-level Penfolds chardonnay, though the acidity is quite strong.

2004 Sarantos Chardonnay $12.95

I'm sure all wineries would like us to think that their grapes were 'soft pressed', so I'm slightly irritated by the 'Soft Press' addition to this Kingston Estate label. That said, the chardonnay from the 2004 vintage is delicate and soft with cedar and ripe fruit flavours – pleasant drinking now.

2004 Trentham Estate 'Murphy's Lore' Chardonnay $11

Just what you'd expect from Trentham's second label –
ripe, fruity, flavoursome, soft, gentle and easy to gulp.

2005 Yalumba 'Oxford Landing' Chardonnay $7.95

A reliable quaffing chardonnay – fresh, clean and well-
made with satiny smooth texture and pleasant fruity
flavours.

RIESLING

As ever, the riesling chapter tends to be one of the strongest in *Quaff*, with a much higher strike rate than any other. It remains the best value quaffing white in Australia. You'll find many of your old favourites reappearing with a new vintage of their wine and, unusually, several rieslings that were recommended last year. Blame the glut and the tremendous competition in retail land. A couple of these are not looking as bright and youthful as they did last year but have other features that make them worthy of consideration.

Five of the wines recommended in this chapter have a recommended retail price of more than $15 – the cut-off point for *Quaff*. We ask wineries to submit wines priced under $15 that are available from October. Those wineries that submit wines with a recommended retail price of more than $15 do so because they believe that the wine is generally available in stores for below $15. I've included those wines because I think you'll appreciate knowing about them.

The reliables –
consistent-quality wines, year in, year out

The Mitchelton 'Blackwood Park' Riesling has appeared in all six editions of *Quaff* and rieslings from Peter Lehmann, Leasingham and Yalumba have appeared in five out of the six editions of *Quaff*. That's consistency!

Buying and Drinking Riesling – Some Tips

Drink bright, young and fresh

Most people enjoy rieslings when they are still in the first flush of youth (essentially within 18 months of harvest) when they are fragrant, fruity and lively with crisp zippy acidity. Last year, most of the rieslings reviewed in this chapter were from the current vintage: that is not the case this year, almost certainly because the wines from 2004 have not yet been sold. However, you can still buy and drink the wines recommended here with confidence. Most of the 2004s are still fresh and lively and where there are signs of development and aging, the wines have other appealing characters.

... or cellar for a few years

If you put riesling away in a cool dark place for a couple of years, it can develop some deliciously interesting bottle-age characters that are well worth exploring. Those with best cellaring potential include the 2004 Peter Lehmann Eden Valley, the 2004 Annie's Lane and the 2004 Taylors.

Screwcap revolution is here

For the first time, all of the rieslings submitted for the *Quaff* tastings were sealed by screwcap (rather than with cork), ensuring that the wine you taste will be exactly as the winemaker intended you to taste it.

BLOODY GOOD

2004 Goundrey 'Homestead' Riesling $14.95

Four strong winds of change are sweeping over Goundrey since their takeover by Canada's Vincor in 2003 and there are signs that wine quality is on the improve. The large volume Homestead range is now sourced entirely from Western Australia and is all the better for that. This was the cheapest and one of the best rieslings which I tasted recently in a line-up from the Mount Barker sub-region: fragrantly floral with a hint of talc, persistent lemon citrus and apple flavours, before a soft, gentle lingering finish. Surprising finesse for a wine at this price point.

2005 Jim Barry Watervale Riesling $13

THE QUAFF 2006 'Whooshable'
WHITE WINE OF THE YEAR AWARD

From an outstanding vintage in the Clare Valley comes this brilliantly priced riesling. It would have been a great year for the Barry family anyway. They bought Australia's most famous vineyard, 'Florita', from Leo Buring in 1986 but had to wait 18 years for the trademark to expire. They have recently celebrated the release of the superb single vineyard 2004 Jim Barry 'The Florita', at $40 a bottle. Since they purchased the Florita vineyard parcels of fruit from the vineyard had made their way into the Watervale wine – alongside grapes from the vineyard that Jim Barry had planted in 1962. So, although this may not be the Florita, it's no surprise that it is once again a very smart wine – and remarkably good value. The 2005 Jim Barry is beautifully floral, has intense lime and lemon juice flavours, wonderful zestiness and a long, dry, zingy finish.

2004 Peter Lehmann Eden Valley Riesling $14.95

Last year, we were spot-on with this superb quaffer –
predicting that it would cellar better than its sibling from
the Barossa. Twelve months on and this is as fresh as an
Eden Valley wildflower (which is much fresher than any
daisy): pristine, showing intense, limey, lemony flavours,
subtle power and great finesse. Great drinking now and a
bargain.

2004 Queen Adelaide Riesling $6.95

This is what *Quaff* is all about: a champ who is boxing
above his (or her?) weight – to pinch a sporting analogy.
Floral aromas, reasonably concentrated lemon and lime
flavours, good weight and length with a drier finish than
most at this price. Value.

2004 Taylors Riesling $17

A dramatic Clare riesling showing the affinity that winemaker Adam Eggins has developed with riesling. It has
good ripeness and intense, pure limey flavours, a tight
structure before a crisp, clean, dry finish.

2004 Wolf Blass 'Eaglehawk' Riesling $12

The competition among the winemakers for the Wolf Blass
riesling grapes must be so intense that it's amazing that a
humbly priced wine like this can be so good. The previous
vintage was very ripe and fruity while this has intense
toasty characters and gentle lingering lemony flavours.

 GOOD

2005 Angoves 'Butterfly Ridge' Riesling $5.95

A more varietal riesling than last year's pretty good offering. This consistent white from the Angoves Riverland
vineyards is a light-bodied lemony citrusy riesling with a
pleasing lift, decent flavours and good length. It's not as
concentrated as some but when you look at the price,
who's grumbling?

2004 Annie's Lane Riesling $17

This Beringer Blass label specialises in making wines from the Clare Valley so it's no surprise that this is regularly one of the stars of the portfolio. There's some development in its deep golden colour, intensity of lime juice flavour and bold, crisp finish.

2004 Chrismont Riesling $13

A delightful quaffer from a King Valley producer that is floral, soft, round and so easy to drink, with lively limey flavours that linger.

2004 Galah Riesling $14.50

The second label for Adelaide Hills producer Stephen George of Ashton Hills is typically restrained, juicy, fine and tight with a pleasing level of extract adding interest and some lanolin characters to the finish.

2004 Jacobs Creek Reserve Riesling $15.95

Not as concentrated as some vintages of this wine but clean, fresh and lemony. Quite dry to finish. Classy.

2005 McWilliams 'Regional Collection' Clare Valley Riesling $18.50

A delicate riesling with pure limey flavours before a powerfully refreshing finish featuring strong limey acidity.

2004 Mitchelton 'Blackwood Park' Riesling $17

One of the very few 'reliables' omnipresent in *Quaff*, which speaks volumes for the consistency of the label and the Goulburn Valley vineyard from which it comes. This vintage was rated Bloody Good last year and is less fragrantly floral and slightly more developed than it was then. Drinking well but not as concentrated as some in the tastings.

2004 Peter Lehmann Barossa Riesling $12

Still available although rated Bloody Good in *Quaff* last year when we thought it should age well. It appears more powerful and more concentrated than it did last year – which you would expect – but seems firmer and broader on the finish. Still a bold, robust white.

2005 Pewsey Vale Riesling $16.95

As ever a terrific value-for-money riesling, especially if you can get it on special. Perhaps, at this stage, it lacks the concentration that it usually has but is zesty and mouth-watering with pure lemony fruit.

2004 Siegersdorf Riesling $9.75

A grand old label for Hardys that has been a consistent performer for *Quaff* offering very good value. There are some talc aromas, lemony flavours with reasonable depth and a dryish, lingering finish.

2004 Wynns Coonawarra Riesling $14.95

The previous vintage of this wine has recently won a trophy at the Sydney Show for Best Value White under $15. It's good to see the show system giving quaffing wines their due. Brian Croser has been their champion – having introduced classes for commercial wines with trophies for the best, firstly in Adelaide, and now in Sydney. The 2003 is no longer the current release but you may be able to find some out their in bottleshop land. At present, Wynns are the most reliable producer of riesling from the area and their wines usually offer very good value. That's certainly the case with this 2004: full-flavoured with lemon blossom aromas, bold lemon citrus flavours and gentle acidity to finish.

▶ PRETTY GOOD

2004 Leasingham 'Bastion' Riesling $14

The entry-level riesling from Hardys' winery based near the township of Clare is clean, fresh and lively with lemon citrus flavours.

2005 McWilliams 'Inheritance' Riesling $7

Some estery aromas, pleasant lemony flavours, gentle refreshing finish.

2004 Palandri Riesling $14.95

Sourced from youngish vines on a leased vineyard at Frankland River, this has intense limeyness with some greenish notes and a fresh, powerful finish.

2004 Penfolds 'Rawsons Retreat' Riesling $9.95

This has good varietal character – limey aromas, lemon citrus flavours. Drink up while it's fresh and lively.

2003 Rosemount Estate 'Diamond Label' Riesling $14.95

As you'd expect, this is looking quite developed. Still, it's limey, powerful, rich and slightly firm on the finish.

2004 Wolf Blass 'Yellow Label' Riesling $14

A well-made riesling with some persistent toastiness and some gentle lemon citrus – a little less concentrated than some.

SAUVIGNON BLANC

Aussies are continuing their love affair with sauvignon blanc as sales continue to rise rapidly in retail shops and restaurants – especially in the cafe/brasserie segment of that market. The Kiwis are doing amazing business, especially with their Marlborough sauvignons, and upmarket restaurants are finding their customers responding well to expensive expressions of the variety from places such as Sancerre in France.

Australia's best sauvignon blancs tend to come from our cooler wine regions (where yields are lower and costs higher) and most of these are priced between $17 and $25. Many represent excellent value for money: try Shaw & Smith, Nepenthe, Geoff Weaver, Alkoomi, Stella Bella, Edwards, Houghton Pemberton, Hanging Rock 'Jim Jim', Bay of Fires or Browns of Padthaway.

There are still bargains to be had for less than $15. However, for the second year in a row, only one in four of the wines tasted is recommended. This suggests that there are too many lacklustre examples of the variety on the market. While clean and fresh, they lacked clear varietal character or any concentration of flavour. In short, they were perfectly good, bland whites. Those that are recommended, of course, tend to be light and bright with intense varietal flavours – even interest and excitement.

The reliables –
consistent-quality wines, year in, year out

The Westend 'Richland' is one of the Reliables having been reviewed in *Quaff* for the sixth consecutive year. It's a remarkable trailblazing performance as most of the other Riverina, or indeed warm area, sauvignons lack intensity and concentration of flavour.

Buying and Drinking Sauvignon Blanc – A Tip

Fresh and lively

In the last three editions of *Quaff*, all the sauvignons that were recommended were current release wines. The deadline for tastings has been kept as late as practical in the year to make it possible for wineries to present the current harvest's offerings. Although we received the same number of wines this year as last year, about half were from the 2004 vintage. Slightly more than half of those reviewed are from that vintage. As producers are asked to forward samples of wines that will be available from November to January, I can only assume that those who haven't moved on to 2005 have yet to sell out of the previous vintage. That accords with what I'm hearing about how tough the market is at present.

Although this is a variety for drinking while it's fresh, young and lively, all of the 2004 sauvignons reviewed here are drinking well at present and should make good summer quaffing.

BLOODY GOOD

2004 Long Flat Wine Company Sauvignon Blanc $11

The new-ish Victorian winery Cheviot Bridge – based in the Yea Valley and bristling with savvy former Mildara Blass marketing executives – bought the Long Flat label from Tyrrells to hasten their move into the American market. It's worked well for them on the Australian market, too, and there have been some terrific bargains under the label – none better than this delicious Adelaide Hill white. The Long Flat Sauvignon has attractive ripe, sweet tropical flavours with some herbal notes, is intense with a silky texture and refreshing, lively, crisp acidity. Great summer drinking.

2004 Mount Trio Sauvignon Blanc $14.90

This is the family label of Gavin Berry, chief winemaker at West Cape Howe, and Gill Graham and is based on their tiny Porongurup vineyard. It has marvellous cool climate intensity, layer after layer of tropical fruit flavours with some minerally notes, taut structure and cleansing acidity, and an aftertaste on which passionfruit lingers. Delicious.

2004 Wangolina Station Sauvignon Blanc $14.95

Sauvignon blanc appears to be the best white varietal coming from the Limestone Coast's Mount Benson – as this excellent quaffer suggests. It's intense, shows pristine tropical fruit and some delicate passionfruit flavours, and refreshing, crisp acidity.

GOOD

2005 Capel Vale 'CV' Sauvignon Blanc $14.95

A repeat performance from this Geographe-based producer for whom Rebecca Caitlin is making some smart wines. There are some tropical flavours with a hint of lime juice. It's zesty and lively and finishes soft and gentle.

2004 Jamiesons Run Sauvignon Blanc $14.95

> Coonawarra often hits the spot with sauvignon blanc. This Beringer Blass-owned winery has done just that with a clean, fresh tropical (gooseberries, lychees) flavoured white that is fresh, vibrant and feels great in the mouth.

▶ PRETTY GOOD

2004 Beresford 'Highwood' SB $14.95

> The same vintage of this McLaren Vale producer's sauvignon reviewed last year hasn't changed in 12 months. Still on the edge, with strong herbal, capsicum flavours. If you enjoy the style . . .

2005 Evans & Tate 'Gnangara' Sauvignon Blanc $13.95

> Clean and fresh with a pleasant mouthfeel and some tropical fruit flavours.

2004 Kingston Sauvignon Blanc $10.95

> Pleasant mouthfeel, soft, round and easy-drinking.

2005 Mitchelton 'Preece' Sauvignon Blanc $14.95

> Pleasant, light-bodied, lightly concentrated green pea characters.

2005 Westend Estate 'Richland' Sauvignon Blanc $10.95

> Clean and lively with green bean, grassy flavours.

SEMILLON

As a varietal white, semillon is pretty much unique to Australia. The style of wine that it produces differs dramatically depending on the part of the country in which it is grown. In New South Wales' Hunter Valley it is a world-class wine that ages brilliantly. Lean, dry and often austere while young, it develops into a mellow, toasty, honeyed classic with time in the bottle. In South Australia's Barossa and Clare Valleys, semillon produces richer, fuller wines with more lemony flavours. In recent times, more wineries in these regions have been moving away from oaked semillons and making fresher, livelier, more drink-now styles. The fresh, herbal, green pea, green bean style that has come out of Western Australia's Margaret River and Great Southern are not represented in this chapter. The better examples of this style sell for more than $15. Anyway, much Western Australian semillon is blended with sauvignon blanc to make a fresh, easy drink-now white blend, which has become enormously popular in cafes, brasseries and restaurants – and the Semillon Sauvignon Blanc chapter.

The reliables –
consistent-quality wines, year in, year out

The Hunter Valley's Tyrrells and the Barossa's Peter Lehmann have been the leading producers of quaffing semillon and have been reviewed in five of the editions of this annual guide. And those two regions have dominated each semillon chapter with Mount Pleasant, Rosemount and Tulloch (in the Hunter), and Bethany and Heritage (in the Barossa) showing recent consistency.

Buying and Drinking Semillon – Some Tips

Each-way bets
I wouldn't recommend more than short term cellar for anyone living in Australia without temperature-controlled conditions. It's just too hot in most places for ideal storage of wine. However, one of the great things about semillon is that you can enjoy it when it's fresh and bouncing with youthful zestiness or leave it for a year or two, by which time it has some gentle, developed, toasty flavours. I think that 'Elizabeth' Semillon (for example) is at its best from seven to 10 years, so holding the 2000 for three years is feasible. Expect it to be pretty impressive then.

Happily unfashionable
Once again, the vast majority of semillons that were submitted to *Quaff* have been reviewed proving that, even though it's unfashionable, the variety makes excellent quality wine under $15. While some would argue that semillon doesn't have the ready appeal and softness of chardonnay or the zippy seductiveness of sauvignon blanc, it does make an ideal partner with food. What may appear austere, and even confronting, when drunk by itself is transformed by the right dish – perhaps fettuccine with a seafood sauce, a Thai or Vietnamese chicken salad, freshly shucked natural oysters ...

▶ BLOODY GOOD

2004 Heritage Semillon $14.95

This is the only wine that Steve Hoff produces at his small family winery in the Barossa Valley and sells for less than the cut-off point of $15. I've always looked forward to tasting the wine because it's invariably excellent value and because the majority of the wines in *Quaff* come from the larger companies. A point of difference is (almost) always refreshing – just like this lively semillon. There's a hint of straw and lanolin aromas. It's full-flavoured and soft with gentle acidity on a clean, dry finish.

2004 McGuigan 'Bin 9000' Semillon $13.95

In a large line-up of Hunter River semillon that I tasted late last year, both the 1999 and the 2004 McGuigan Bin 9000 performed extraordinarily well. I gave a gold medal to the 1999, which has won a swag of trophies, and marked the 2004 at 18.0 – a fabulous score for such a young wine. You could have knocked me over with the proverbial feather when the identity of the wines – and their price – was revealed. They were the cheapest of the 70 wines tasted and among the best. There are small quantities of the 1999 at cellar door – at the same *low* price as the 2004. The younger semillon has intense lime and lemongrass flavour with some slatey, minerally characters, is clean and fresh, and finishes with zippy, juicy acidity.

2000 Mount Pleasant 'Elizabeth' Semillon $18

Value rarely gets better than this. Few Aussie whites have a more glorious lineage than the 'Elizabeth' Semillon. When it's young, the wines are light, fine and intense with bright lemony zesty acidity. With some bottle age these marvellous unoaked wines shed their youth and reveal mellow toasty honeyed flavours before a gently complex finish. Best of all, McWilliams make them in huge quantities at their Mount Pleasant winery in the Hunter and so the price is kept within the realms of the affordable. You should be able to find them on special for less than $15: otherwise imagine you saw this in the over $15 chapter. It's vibrant, intense, youthful with freshly squeezed lime juice and some herbal notes before a typically crisp, dry finish.

2004 Peter Lehmann Semillon $12

Perhaps this doesn't have the intense toastiness or sheer class of the 2002: perhaps it has a bit less concentration of flavour than the 2003. However, it does have the lively freshness that was such a delightful feature of the 2003 and some of the floral notes that the 2002 showed early in its life. In summary, this is another excellent vintage from one of the Barossa's best producers of unoaked semillon – or just about anything vinous. (It was last year's *Quaff* Winery of the Year.)

 GOOD

2004 Bethany Semillon $14

For the second year in a row this semillon from the Schrapel family – long-term residents of the Barossa – has been rated Good. Set in the vicinity of the hamlet of Bethany, the winery is a favourite of mine because the Bethany hillscape – vineyard and winery – adorns the cover of each of the books in my wife, Elaine's, *Eden Glassie* series. As each book takes part at a different time of the year, the covers show Bethany in the four seasons. I know this is a shameless plug but Elaine did finish the quartet this year and it's the first time that a children's book (or series of books) has been set on a vineyard. By the way, the 2004 Bethany Semillon has lovely juiciness, pleasant grassy flavours and a dry, cleansing finish featuring lemony acidity.

2003 Rosemount Estate 'Diamond Label' Semillon $14.95

An unoaked Hunter Valley semillon from one of the regulars in this chapter. It has just a hint of the development you'd expect from a two-year-old white: pristine grassy flavours persist.

2004 Tulloch Semillon $13.95

Less austere and confronting than the 2003 Tulloch, this is softer and has a much more pleasant mouthfeel. There are lanolin and grassy flavours, which build in the mouth and linger. Dry, crisp and gentle.

2004 Tyrrells 'Old Winery' Semillon $11.95

> The 2004 Qantas/Gourmet Traveller WINE Winemaker of the Year, Andrew Spinaze, is a semillon wiz so it's scarcely surprising that even the Tyrrells' cheapie represents great value. It's fragrant, has lifted lanolin characters with some lemony notes, good intensity of flavour and refreshing lively acidity.

➤ PRETTY GOOD

2003 Lilyvale 'Silver Downs' Semillon $15

> A fresh, clean and grassy semillon from a new Queensland producer – marred by some bitterness on the finish.

2004 Parri Semillon $14.95

> From a new-ish family winery situated in South Australia's Fleurieu Peninsula: it is restrained, clean and has a pleasing mouthfeel before powerful acidity.

2004 Saltram 'Makers Table' Semillon $10

> Fresh and lively with clean, grassy flavours: fair value.

VERDELHO AND OTHER WHITE VARIETALS

This chapter focuses on white varietals other than the classics: chardonnay, riesling, semillon and sauvignon blanc. By far the most popular of these is verdelho, followed by chenin blanc, pinot gris (or pinot grigio) and viognier. These are mainly aromatic varieties and do particularly well in warmer regions: along the Murray River, in the Swan Valley, in Queensland, in the Hunter Valley, in McLaren Vale and along Langhorne Creek. These are made without the influence of oak and can be bottled soon after vintage, so they tend to be reasonably priced.

There has been a prolonged rise in the popularity of verdelho in the past five years or so – mainly because of its success on cafe and brasserie wine lists where its drinkability and ripe flavours make it hard to resist. The success of the sweet Amberley Estate Chenin Blanc has spawned many who seek to share that popularity. I'm not a great fan of the style, although when it's as good as the 2005 Houghton, I'm impressed.

Pinot grigio and viognier have been the most successful of the exotic varieties that have become available in the past decade. Both of these experienced huge leaps in the volume produced in the 2005 vintage – pinot grigio up 162 per cent to 5492 tonnes and viognier up 36 per cent to 5324 tonnes.

The reliables –
consistent-quality wines, year in, year out

After six editions of *Quaff*, only two wines have appeared in this chapter on each occasion and both are rated Bloody Good for 2005. They are the Moondah Brook Verdelho and the Tahbilk Marsanne – consistently excellent value-for-money wines.

Buying and Drinking Verdelho and Other White Varietals – A Tip

Fresh is best

The tough retail environment has meant that sales of white wine are slower than expected in some segments of the market and that's reflected in several chapters. Not so here, which – as expected – is dominated by whites from the most recent harvest. The freshness, vitality and ripe, full-on flavour are very much part of the joy that the best of these wines can impart.

BLOODY GOOD

2005 Beelgara Estate '11.05' Pinot Grigio $14.95

This reincarnation of the Rosetto family winery in the Riverina continues to impress in the *Quaff* tastings. I suspect that the wine's name comes from the amount of alcohol that it contains. This has floral aromas, a lovely mouthfeel, bright fruity flavours, smooth sensuous texture, good weight and a crisp, clean finish.

2005 Houghton Chenin Blanc $10.50

A wonderfully aromatic varietal – its attractive floral and tropical notes are alluring and many will love its soft, round, viscous texture and full fruity flavour. Those who love some sweetness will be delighted by the wine, while those who want more zingy, dry crispness on the finish should look elsewhere.

2005 Moondah Brook Verdelho $12

One of the Reliables hits the high spots once more. Included, with distinction, for a record equalling sixth time, this is a fantastic summer wine that is light, bright and fragrant with lively grassy flavours and a hint of passionfruit. Fresh, pristine and zingy, it finishes crisp, zesty and long.

2005 Tahbilk Marsanne $14.90

Another of the rare band of Reliables that has featured in all six editions of *Quaff*. From the Goulburn Valley and the world's largest planting of marsanne comes this delightful fruity white, which is fresh and lively, has a pleasant mouth-feel and tingly, zesty acidity to finish. Ages beautifully.

2005 Trentham Estate 'La Famiglia' Pinot Grigio $14.95

A delightful Aussie example of pinot grigio from Tony Murphy and his family at Mildura. It is fragrant in a tanta-lising way, has heaps of spicy character, some savouriness, and a finish that lingers.

2005 Woop Woop Verdelho $12.95

This is a collaboration of the ubiquitous winemaker Ben Riggs and Tony Parkinson, owner of Pennys Hill in McLaren Vale. It's hard to ignore the name or the label: the wine is delicious, so just sit back and *Quaff* on. There are heaps of tropical fruit aromatics, zippy, vibrant honey-suckle flavours, and a clean, crisp finish. Priced to sell, too.

2005 Yalumba 'Y Series' Viognier $11.95

Rated Bloody Good once again, Yalumba have repeated their triumph of last year with a subtle white that has deli-cate aromatics (a hint of dried apricots), gentle viscosity, good weight, and a pristine, fresh flavour that lingers. It's a food wine, so try with stir-fried prawns or lightly spiced lobster.

2004 Zilzie Viognier $14.95

When it won a gold medal at the 2005 International Wine and Spirit Competition in London, the judges described it as being 'deliciously long with tropical fruit notes all the way'. In Australia, the wine has won a trophy and gold medal at the Riverland Show and gold at the Hobart Show. Not bad for a wine that sells for under $15. I, too, liked the wine. It's quite restrained on the nose, although the palate shows good varietal character: musk and dried apricot fruitiness with a pleasant viscous texture as well as some delicious juiciness. I loved the previous vintage, too. It's good to see that Zilzie are capable of consistency with this new grape variety.

 GOOD

2004 Angoves 'Stonegate' Verdelho $7.95

In a great year such as 2005, the Riverland can produce some remarkable bargains – like this lively quaffer. It is clean and fresh, has tropical fruit and passionfruit flavours and crisp acidity.

2004 Brown Brothers Pinot Grigio $15.90

A touch over the $15 price point, but often under it on special, this is a terrific white from one of Australia's favourite family wineries. It's an excellent expression of this trendy new grape variety – and much better priced than most you'll find on the market. There are some delicate savoury flavours, pleasing viscous texture, and refreshing slatey acidity. Best with food: say, a lightly spiced Vietnamese chicken salad.

2005 Coriole Chenin Blanc $14.50

A regular in *Quaff.* Chenin seems to do well in McLaren Vale. It's bright, vibrant, has green pea and grassy flavours and a zesty, refreshing finish.

2005 Dowie Doole Chenin Blanc $15.50

A quinella of McLaren Vale favourites: fruity, herby flavours; lifted aromatics; tropical notes on a zippy finish.

2004 Evans & Tate 'Gnangara' Chenin Blanc $13.95

While this looks to me much more like gewürztraminer than chenin – muscaty fragrance, sweet rose petal flavours – it will appeal widely to those who enjoy some sweetness and character in their whites.

2004 Lindemans Reserve Verdelho $12.95

This vintage was rated Bloody Good last year so I'm surprised to see it still available. Perhaps that shows how tough the market is. It still has the vibrance and freshness that made it so attractive last year although without the same intense green pea, green bean primary flavours. Instead, there's some grassy characters without the tropical lift that it showed earlier on.

2004 T'Gallant 'Juliet' Pinot Grigio $14.95

Sourced from the Mornington Peninsula, this is a bit more subtle than many of the wines in this chapter. It has good weight so appears plumper, has delicate apple and pear flavours, and a long, gentle finish. Will be lifted by subtle, spicy food, such as Thai fish cakes.

2004 Zonte's Footstep Verdelho $14.95

That Ben Riggs again. This time sourcing fruit from a 210 hectare vineyard in Langhorne Creek with the syndicate that includes Geoff Hardy, John Pargeter and Zar Brooks. It's a good quaffer – well-made, fresh, light-bodied with cool apple and pear flavours and crisp refreshing acidity.

▶ PRETTY GOOD

2005 Bleasdale Verdelho $13.50

Verdelho is Langhorne Creek's best white: this is fresh, clean and lively with pleasant grassy flavours.

2004 Clovely Estate 'Left Field' Verdelho $14.95
>Verdelho has done well in Queensland and so it's great to see this fresh, clean, flavoursome white featured in *Quaff*.

2004 Kingston Estate Verdelho $13.95
>A pleasant, refreshing drink.

2004 McGuigan 'Black Label' Verdelho $9.95
>A restrained Hunter Valley verdelho that is clean, fresh and lively.

2005 McPherson Verdelho $8.95
>A fresh, clean and lively quaffer, straightforward and pleasant: comes with the additional personal recommendation of my mate, Kingsley Sullivan, the New Norcia baker.

2005 Moondah Brook Verdelho $12
>A good drink – clean, fresh and pleasant, easy-drinking – but lacks the usual intensity of this aromatic varietal.

2005 Paul Conti 'The Tuarts' Chenin Blanc $14.95
>Long-established family winery in the Swan District, which has produced this lively, grassy chenin that will make pleasant summer drinking.

2005 Sirromet Verdelho $14.40
>From Queensland's largest producer – situated at Mount Cotton about 45 minutes from Brisbane and worth the trip if you are in the area – comes a light-bodied verdelho that is fresh and lively with a zingy, crisp finish.

2005 Tyrrells Verdelho $9.95
>Another fresh, clean grassy Hunter verdelho with zippy, crisp acidity.

SEMILLON CHARDONNAY BLENDS

Some believe that this unique Aussie blend succeeds because it places the magically popular word 'chardonnay' on the label and delivers decent quaffing wines at everyday prices. Certainly anything with chardonnay in it sells. The best of these blends effectively combines the fresh grassy flavours of semillon and its mid-palate weight with the richer, more overtly ripe, peachy, melony flavours and soft mouthfeel of chardonnay. They tend to be dryer on the finish than many whites at the price point.

The reliables –
consistent-quality wines, year in, year out
The only example of this blend to appear in each of the six editions of *Quaff* is the Rosemount Estate Semillon Chardonnay, clearly marking Rosemount as a producer of this style in which you can have the utmost confidence. Penfolds, with their 'Koonunga Hill' and 'Rawsons Retreat' labels, are also a safe bet.

Buying and Drinking Semillon Chardonnay Blends – Some Tips

Drinkability, affordability

The best example of a semillon chardonnay blend that I can remember was a Peter Lehmann Shareholders Reserve that I tasted – and drank – at the winery in the Barossa Valley. It was a beautifully crafted and intensely flavoured white that featured rich, concentrated fruit and classy (and expensive) cedary oak. Semillon chardonnay blends of this quality are rare. Sometimes there is an oak influence on these blends – Penfolds 'Koonunga Hill' is matured in one-, two- and three-year-old barrels, and Blues Point obviously has contact with oak – and this can give the blend additional depth of flavour. Most are unoaked and therefore semillon chardonnays are drinkable and affordable (important for lovers of the style). They seem to slip down all too easily.

Love the Murray River

For me, the most significant Australian environmental issue of the times is the need to improve the flow of the Murray River. We believe that responsible viticulture is compatible with this aim. Technological developments – even something as simple as moving from overhead sprinklers to drip irrigation – in many vineyards along the Murray (in regions such as the Riverland, Murray–Darling and Swan Hill) have significantly reduced the volume of water used. These irrigated regions provide most of the grapes for semillon chardonnay blends. Not only do the abundant sunshine and warm growing conditions give the wines ripe, generous flavours but they help to keep the cost of production down. And we all love that.

▶ BLOODY GOOD

2004 Rosemount Estate Semillon Chardonnay $10.95

Epitomises the blend: fresh, clean and lively – in fact, vibrant – with a pleasing mouthfeel and crisp, dry finish.

▄▄▶ GOOD

2004 Blues Point Chardonnay Semillon $10.95

Gentle cedary oak dominates on the nose and palate but gives the wine character. Has some vibrance.

2004 Penfolds 'Rawsons Retreat' Semillon Chardonnay $10.95

Similar in style to the previous vintage: fresh, clean, lively with pleasant, persistent, grassy flavours.

2004 Peter Lehmann Semillon Chardonnay $12

Some intense grassy characters, good mouthfeel, clean, dry finish.

2004 Red Deer Station Semillon Chardonnay $12.95

This label of Griffith-based newcomer, Dal Broi, presents a soft, round, easy-drinking white that is pleasant in the mouth and is fresh and bright.

▄▄▶ PRETTY GOOD

2004 Andrew Garrett 'Garrett' Semillon Chardonnay $11

Fresh, clean and dry with gentle flavours.

2004 Beelgara Estate 'Silky Oak' Semillon Chardonnay $8

Clean, well-made with light, grassy flavours.

2004 Lindemans 'Cawarra' Semillon Chardonnay $6.95

Same wine as recommended last year: still pleasant in the mouth with more noticeable grassy flavours and soft, gentle acidity.

NV Matthew Lang Semillon Chardonnay $5.45

Recommended again, this year looking brighter and fresher with some lanolin character, good weight and pleasant dry finish.

2004 Penfolds 'Koonunga Hill' Semillon Chardonnay $14.95
> Fresh and clean with pleasant flavours and crisp, dry finish.

2004 Pump Hill Semillon Chardonnay $7.95
> A second label for Roberts Estate, which has lifted grassy flavours, is fresh, bright and lively with a pleasant mouth-feel.

SEMILLON SAUVIGNON BLANC BLENDS

It wouldn't be difficult to accept any claim that the Margaret River winemakers made that they had invented this style. Semillon from this region has a grassy character that bears an amazing resemblance to sauvignon blanc, much more so than in other areas. Combining the two varieties seemed a natural thing to do as the weight, fullness and complexity of semillon added a dimension to the vibrant juiciness of sauvignon blanc. The blend was a much more satisfying drink than either of the two components.

Because of its popularity, most of the good examples of the blend from Margaret River have moved above $15 and their place has been taken by producers in the cooler areas of Western Australia – especially Pemberton and Frankland River – where the grapes are cheaper and, in many cases, zingier.

The important thing about this blend is having a fresh, zesty sauvignon blanc component. Many producers will get this by sourcing sauvignon blanc (or at least some of it) from a cool region. Those who rely on fruit from a warmer region aim to pick it early to retain that lively acidity that adds sparkle to the blend. Plenty of other regions have taken up the challenge and are producing fresh, lively, uncomplicated whites from these varieties. The Adelaide Hills and Orange are two places that impress.

The reliables –
consistent-quality wines, year in, year out

Two labels – the Houghton Semillon Sauvignon Blanc and the Plantagenet Hazard Hill Semillon Sauvignon Blanc – have now appeared in five of the last six editions of *Quaff*, making them reliable buys and consistent good value.

The previous three vintages of the Houghton have also been outstanding – of gold medal quality – making this arguably Australia's best value white over the last four years.

Buying and Drinking Semillon Sauvignon Blanc Blends – Some Tips

An each-way drink

For me, wine is almost invariably an accompaniment to food. There are, of course, times when you'll want to relax with a refreshing glass of wine – on a quiet summer's afternoon or at a wild party. On those occasions, sem sav blancs are the ideal drink. They are also the perfect wine to serve with fresh salads, noodles, pasta or Asian-style fish or chicken dishes because they are suited to light, uncomplicated dishes. For this reason, they are very well represented on cafe and brasserie lists across the country.

Affordable quaffers

The trendiest and the best of the semillon sauvignon blends do tend to creep up in price, although some of these can sometimes be found on special at below $15. I was particularly impressed by the 2005 Cape Vale CV, the 2004 Palandri and the 2004 Juniper Crossing – see Whites over $15 (page 173): snap them up if you can find them at a good price. Having said that, there will always be plenty of good semillon sauvignon blancs at quaffing prices. They are cheap to make because they don't need oak maturation and can be ready for bottling and distribution within a few months of harvest.

➤ BLOODY GOOD

2004 Cartwheel Sauvignon Blanc Semillon $14.95

Following the success that Beringer Blass has had with its Eden Valley label, Shadowood, when it was launched last year, they have weighed in with a Western Australian label, Cartwheel. The giant wine company has long had designs on Margaret River and has been keen to get a toehold in the west. So popular are the Margaret River wines on the Sydney market that Beringer Blass believes that having some of the region's product in their portfolios is useful as an icebreaker when their reps are calling on retail and on-premises customers, at least in Harbour City. Winemaker Sam Glaetzer has been nurturing the project for two years and has come up with two levels of wines: a Margaret River range priced about $22 and Western Australian blends priced between $15 and $17. This vibrant white is sourced from Frankland River and made at Ferngrove under Sam Glaetzer's direction. It has clean tropical fruit flavours (gooseberry, lychee, passionfruit) and refreshing natural acidity.

2005 Four Sisters Sauvignon Blanc Semillon $14.90

This is by far the best wine I've seen under this reliable label, part-owned and made by Mt Langhi Ghiran wine-maker Trevor Mast. It has a sweet floral bouquet, is soft, round and delicious, oh-so-easy to drink with its ripe trop-ical fruit flavours and a crisp, clean finish.

2005 Houghton Semillon Sauvignon Blanc $11.95

Now that is consistency! Rated Bloody Good in all editions of *Quaff* since the unique rating system was introduced – four years in a row. And it's won trophies and gold medals galore in the Western Australian show system, consistently thrashing much more expensive wines. How do the team at Houghton do it? Vineyard resources and skilful wine-making, I guess. It has intense tropical fruit flavours (lychee, gooseberry and passionfruit) with hints of cut grass and fresh herbs, vibrance and zestiness before a crisp, zingy finish. A quintessential expression of this blend that Western Australia seems to have made its own.

2005 Leaping Lizard Semillon Sauvignon Blanc $14

A second label for the Frankland River winery Ferngrove, which has scored back-to-back Bloody Goods – and therefore going for a third in *Quaff 2007*. This year, it was marginally preferred to the Ferngrove – the *Quaff* White Wine of the Year in 2005. There's a lively zestiness, pristine fruit flavours, some grassiness and fresh garden herb characters, before a vibrant, lingering finish.

2004 Nepenthe 'Tryst' Sauvignon Blanc Semillon $12.95

This medium-sized Adelaide Hills producer has a budget-priced (for the Adelaide Hills) red and this white labelled as 'Tryst'. The Sauvignon Blanc Semillon blend has heaps of rich, ripe, intense gooseberry, guava and tropical fruit characters almost bursting out of the glass. It's vibrant, full of flavour, and finishes with refreshing, zingy, dry acidity.

GOOD

2005 Ferngrove Sauvignon Blanc Semillon $14.95

This was tasted pretty early in its life, so the wine may develop further as it settles down, but not quite as brilliant or intense as the 2004 vintage. Still, this is a very good example of the style: lifted grassy characters, hints of tropical fruit and passionfruit, clean, refreshing acidity to finish.

2004 Logan 'Apple Tree Flat' Semillon Sauvignon Blanc $9.95

What a difference a year can make to these 'drink-early' style whites. This vintage was rated Bloody Good in last year's *Quaff* and scored a rave review. I liked it in this year's tasting but felt it lacked the vitality that it showed last year and the intense passionfruit and guava flavours. I retasted the wine once I knew that it was a rave wine from Orange, but still thought it lacked the zip and zing that I saw last year. Still, I'm mightily impressed with the Logan family wines (great sauvignon for $18), so look for the 2005 vintage and remember that this still represents good value.

2005 Long Flat Semillon Sauvignon Blanc $8.95

The label was bought from Tyrrells a few years ago to spearhead Cheviot Bridge's drive onto the export market. There's some freshness from the very good 2005 vintage, good mouthfeel and lively, cleansing acidity.

2005 McPherson Semillon Sauvignon Blanc $8.95

This large Goulburn Valley producer has a much greater presence on the American market than it has domestically but it's working on that. This needs a couple of swirls to clean it up on the nose. The palate is clean, fresh and the mouthfeel is pleasant.

2005 McWilliams 'Inheritance' Semillon Sauvignon Blanc $7

Great value from this McWilliams cheapie: ripe, sweet tropical fruit flavours, quite intense, straightforward but good drinking.

2005 Penfolds 'Koonunga Hill' Semillon Sauvignon Blanc $14.95

Intense varietal character – grassy, herbal flavours – gives this white blend some appeal. It's vibrant, bright and easy-drinking.

▶ PRETTY GOOD

2004 Crofters Semillon Sauvignon Blanc $16

This also needed a swirl to clean it up but, that done, it showed as an impressive racy white with green bean, herbal flavours and a crisp, dryish finish.

2004 Evans & Tate Margaret River Sauvignon Blanc Semillon $13.50

Margaret River's largest producer has done well with this blend for many years: lively, punchy, summery – intense passionfruit flavours are a highlight.

2004 Goundrey 'Homestead' Sauvignon Blanc Semillon $14.95

From the large Mount Barker-based winery, which is showing improved performance: a clean, fresh, light-bodied white with a pleasant mouthfeel – in the softer style.

2004 Hazard Hill Semillon Sauvignon Blanc $12

Big selling second label for Plantagenet and one of the reliables in this section: restrained on the nose, fresh, clean and lively on the palate.

2005 Yellowtail Semillon Sauvignon Blanc $9.95

A pleasant light-bodied white from Australia's greatest export success – based at Griffith on the Riverina. This is fresh, clean and has a pleasant mouthfeel.

OTHER WHITE BLENDS

There's no question that I gulp when I learn the composition of some of the unusual blends that I taste for this chapter. Because of the price point that is being targeted, these are bin-end wines. So everything goes in. The amazing thing is that they often taste so good.

It's important for readers of the book to know that blind tastings are part and parcel of *Quaff*. As I don't know what the blends are until after I have finished making notes on the wines and rating them, I can't be put off by my expectations of what a seemingly bizarre combination of grapes might produce. I remember the first time that I tasted a chardonnay verdelho. I thought then Houghton winemaker, Paul Lapsley, had taken leave of his senses. The wine was delicious. And the blend remains part of the Houghton portfolio – and is, once again, reviewed in *Quaff*. Surprise packets this year include the Fishbone blend of semillon and chenin, and the 'La Biondina' colombard, sauvignon blanc, riesling. Somehow, they work.

Thank goodness Australian appellation laws allow for blending literally any grape from anywhere with any other grape from anywhere else. What is pleasing, too, is that these blends still express a good sense of where they're from – whether it be the grassy, fresh, perfumed quality of the Western Australian blends or the ripe, rich flavours of the warmer-climate South Australian wines.

The reliables –
consistent-quality wines, year in, year out

Only one wine in this chapter has appeared in all six editions of *Quaff* – the Primo Estate 'La Biondina'. In the process, it's moved to this chapter from Other White Varietals – where it shone as a straight colombard. From the 2004 vintage, it has been a blend of colombard, sauvignon blanc and riesling. As consistent and good as ever. Other consistent performers include Rosemount Estate and Hougthon.

Buying and Drinking Other White Blends – Some Tips

Fresh is best

There is no question that the fresher these blends are the better they are. All these wines are either from 2004 or 2005. They need to be drunk up before they are two years old, when their fruit flavours are at their liveliest and brightest. In fact, they are generally at their best before they have had their first birthday.

Warm weather wines

Most of the blends we recommend come from warm (or warmish) climate grape-growing regions such as the Barossa, Margaret River and the regions along the Murray. They are full of ripe fruit flavours, and this gives you a clue as to when to drink them: they're all very much summer quaffers. They are straightforward, flavoursome wines – no pretensions, no complexities. Drink and enjoy.

▄▶ BLOODY GOOD

2004 Cape Mentelle 'Georgiana' $14.95

Named for pioneer and naturalist Georgiana Molloy, this is a bin-end blend from Margaret River. In 2004 it's sauvignon blanc, chardonnay, semillon and chenin blanc. The sauvignon flavours dominate, so it has rich, concentrated ripe tropical fruit flavours, with some green, herby notes. This is a vibrant white blend, which is crisp, clean, zesty and refreshing.

2005 Fishbone Classic White $14.95

The producers have chosen to identify this second label of Blackwood Wines as coming from Western Australia rather than its pretty much unknown region of Blackwood Valley (among the tall timbers of Western Australia's south-west). The semillon chenin blanc blend works surprisingly well – it's all ripe tropical fruits, vibrant passionfruit and pineapple flavours before a crisp, clean finish with lingering passionfruit. Delicious.

2004 Palandri 'Baldivis' Classic Dry White $11.95

This Baldivis label of Western Australian producer, Palandri, often offers excellent value – as it does with this fruity white. Heaps of ripe tropical fruit (white peach, pear, lychee, passionfruit) make it a satisfying summer drink.

2004 Rosemount Estate 'Jigsaw' Riesling Fronti Verdelho $7.95

Hugely appealing aromatic white that has intense grapey, muscaty, musky flavours, thick viscous texture and a touch of sweetness on the finish.

🍾 GOOD

2005 Elderton 'Ashmead Family' Sauvignon Blanc Verdelho $13.95

For the second year running this family winery from the Barossa has done well with this flavoursome white blend. As with the best of these blends, there's mountains of overt tropical fruit flavours. This, however, has a tighter structure than most and so it's racy and taut, has some intensity and good length.

2005 Primo Estate 'La Biondina' $14

The genial Joe Grilli decided to tweak this wine – although not change the style – from the 2004 vintage. Instead of a varietal (100 per cent) colombard, he added some Adelaide Hills sauvignon blanc and Eden Valley riesling to make a unique blend for the wine he has long called 'La Biondina' (the young blonde). There's plenty of tropical fruits (guava, passionfruit) that lift the bouquet of the 2005, while the palate shows similar tropical notes and some green fruit characters before a crisp, refreshing finish.

🍾 PRETTY GOOD

2004 Angove's 'Butterfly Ridge' Colombard Chardonnay $5.95

This is clean, fresh, reasonably fruity and perfectly straightforward. Not bad at the price.

2004 Chain of Ponds 'Novello Bianco' Semillon Pinot Grigio $14.25

While it needed a vigorous swirl to clean up the nose, I enjoyed its viscosity and savoury dried herb flavours.

2005 Crocodile Creek 'Undercurrent' $11.95

This is a pleasant fruity wine that is reasonably dry.

2004 Houghton Chardonnay Verdelho $11

This has become a Houghton favourite at the price point: intense tropical fruit and passionfruit flavours that linger.

2005 Houghton White Burgundy $10.50

This is one of Western Australia's best selling whites and has been made continuously since 1937. Usually it's a great quaffer but it didn't show as well in our tastings as I'd expect: pretty good but not one of its best vintages. It might be a bit too young and so may get better with a few months in the bottle. Clean, fresh and lively with gentle passionfruit characters.

2004 Queen Adelaide Classic Dry White $7

Beginning to tire a little but a pleasant mouthful with stone fruit flavours.

2005 Sandalford 'Element' Classic White $12.50

This is a blend of Western Australian chenin (37 per cent), verdelho (30 per cent) semillon (22 per cent) – don't ask about the rest. It's well made, soft and gentle with fresh passionfruit flavours.

2004 Snowy Creek Chenin Blanc Verdelho $6

A cheapie from the Victorian Alps: fresh, clean and pleasantly drinkable.

2004 Zilzie 'Buloke Reserve' Classic Dry White $9.95

Fruity, ripe tropical flavours, clean, crisp acidity. Straightforward but pleasant.

Pretty in pink

Rosés under $15

PINK WINES UNDER $15

The rosé revolution continues to gather strength. A huge leap in its popularity was apparent last year as it resulted in a doubling of the number of rosés we recommended. This year the number is up slightly in this chapter but there's been a dramatic increase in the number of rosés I'm recommending over $15. This pretty much fits in with the samples that I've received: about the same number as last year in the under $15 price bracket and a giant leap in the number of samples for my general new release tastings. I tasted more than 70 rosés for the book – a number undreamt of a couple of years ago – and there are more out there. Many wineries are making a rosé for cellar door sales only, so if you love the style, look for them when you are out and about exploring the wine trails.

Below $15, the majority of rosés have some residual sugar to flesh out and smooth the palate and to make them easier to drink. This style is enormously popular. If you prefer your rosés dry, then there are plenty recommended in *Quaff 2006*.

Like so many of the wines that are produced to be drunk early, screwcaps are becoming increasingly prevalent. We applaud the continued use of screwcaps with almost all rosés – this year all but one (Hardy's) of the Australian rosés in the under $15 price bracket had screwcaps. This means that vibrant youthful freshness will be part of your experience of drinking rosé.

Buying and Drinking Rosés – Some Tips

Fresh is best

I'm a great believer that rosés are best drunk young and so am a bit surprised that such a high proportion of the wines that I've recommended this year are from the 2004 vintage. The most likely reason for this is that wineries hadn't moved on to the latest vintage in time for the *Quaff* tastings and weren't planning to move on before Christmas 2005. Remember that we ask our producers to only send us wines that will be available at least a few months after *Quaff* appears. While this is no cause for alarm, as rosés do have light fine tannins to enable them to keep in the short term, keep your eyes peeled for the change of vintage. When in doubt, remember that fresh is best.

Think pink revolution

While more rosés are more widely available in Australia than ever before – and rosés are the fastest growing segment of the market in Britain at the moment – this is not time for complacency. Support those winemakers who have been overwhelmed by the tide of public opinion and given us what we wanted. More choice: more rosés. Continue supporting the rosés push!

▰▶ BLOODY GOOD

2004 Capel Vale Duck $14.95

Rosé has become wonderfully popular in Australia in the last year or two – after being considered so unfashionable that the Rosé Liberation Army was formed to promote its virtues. Capel Vale winemaker, Rebecca Catlin, has produced a little beauty from unfashionable Pemberton shiraz, which has a superb vermilion colour, is soft, round and almost lush with some spicy, plummy characters, good concentration of flavour and a finish of considerable length with a touch of sweetness. Top gold at the Vintage Cellars 2004 National Wine Show in Canberra. The 2005, also sourced from Capel Vale's Sheldrake vineyard at Pemberton, has musk stick aromas, is soft, round and gently flavoured with some sweetness on its lively finish.

2004 Kangaroo Ridge 'The Aussie' White Shiraz $6.95

I found it hard to believe when the labels were revealed and I learnt the identity of this second label from Cowra Estate. I know! I know! As if white shiraz weren't bad enough for a serious wine chappie like myself. But 'The Aussie' on top of 'Kangaroo Ridge' nearly had me weeping in my spit bucket. Worst of all, I liked the wine. And at the price, it's a bargain. There's not much aroma, the palate is noticeably drier than the Cowra rosé with some strawberry and savoury characters, the texture is quite viscous, and the aftertaste is pleasant.

2004 Scarpantoni 'Ceres' Rosé $14

A very good McLaren Vale rosé made from gamay: soft, round and fruity with strawberry and raspberry flavours and a crispness on the finish that balances the sweetness. This also scored Bloody Good last year, but I've tried it blind twice recently and it's still drinking beautifully.

2005 Taylors 'Promised Land' White Cabernet $13.95

A terrific Clare Valley rosé that is fragrant, soft and round with juicy strawberry flavours, some sweetness and a crisp, refreshing finish.

 GOOD

2004 Cowra Estate Cabernets Rosé $13.79

This is a light-bodied rosé that shows some strawberry characters and a hint of stalkiness. It is soft, round and very easy-drinking thanks to its mid-palate sweetness.

2004 Deakin Rosé $10

This is the kind of vibrant, juicy rosé that can be enjoyed at the height of summer or even as we start to light up the autumn fires. It has clean, fresh strawberry flavours, and wonderful vibrancy before a pleasantly dryish finish. An excellent wine from the Murray–Darling near Mildura, the engine room of the Australian industry.

2005 Jacobs Creek Shiraz Rosé $9.95

A vibrant rosé with bright strawberry and raspberry characters that is filled out by a hint of sweetness. It has good weight and depth of flavour.

2004 Jingalla Cabernet Rouge $13

This is from a small Porongurup vineyard in deepest Great Southern. It's a light-bodied cabernet sauvignon, which is darker in colour than most rosés, has an attractive floral bouquet and red berry characters. It has heaps of flavour and will appeal to those who like their rosés very sweet. Ages surprisingly well.

2005 Moondah Brook Cabernet Rosé $12.95

A delicious rosé from one of the most popular labels of Western Australia's largest producer, Houghton. It is bright pink in colour, has floral fragrances, is bright, clean and lively with a modest touch of sweetness held in check by crisp acidity.

➤ PRETTY GOOD

2005 Angoves 'Nine Vines' Rosé $14

This blend of grenache and shiraz is fragrant, shows intense raspberry characters, is fresh, clean and sweet with cleansing acidity.

2005 Jane Brook 'Plain Jane' Rosé $12.50

A sweetish rosé sourced from Margaret River by this long-established Swan Valley producer. It has a light pink colour, strawberry and red cherry flavours, is soft and round with a very pleasant finish.

2004 Lindemans 'Bin 35' Rosé $8.95

This is a light-bodied, sweet rosé with boiled lolly, fairy floss, confected characters. It is soft, round and easy-drinking and will appeal to many – especially at the price.

2005 Mount Hurtle Grenache Rosé $8.95

A soft, juicy rosé from McLaren Vale's Geoff Merrill. It has fleshy, plummy flavours and is drier than most at this price point. Good value.

2005 Tall Poppy 'Select' Rosé $7.95

There are some confect, spun sugar characters here, especially on the nose. The palate is fresh, spicy and lively and the sweetness is held in reasonable check.

2004 Tobacco Road Rosé $11

From the King Valley, and so a reminder of one of the crops that provided many families in the region with a livelihood in times past, this has some green herbal notes, a rich, soft berry mid-palate, and sweetness that is balanced by strong acidity.

Barbecue wines

Red wines under $15

CABERNET SAUVIGNON

This is one of the toughest sections of *Quaff* in which to get a favourable review, with only three wines getting a Bloody Good rating and only 18 being recommended – out of nearly 70 tasted. Part of the problem is that the variety's high levels of tannin (the drying grippiness you feel on the sides of your tongue and gums) can make the wines a little sturdy, even confronting – especially when compared to more supple, fleshy, and less firmly tannic varieties such as shiraz and grenache.

Cabernet sauvignon has declined in popularity in the last few years and is certainly a much harder sell now than it used to be. The reality is that it is one of the classic wines of the world, does particularly well in many parts of Australia, and makes many brilliant wines – at all price points. That's why the best wines in the chapter are well worth considering. I've talked to plenty of producers in the past year who've admitted that they've dropped the price of their cabernet in order to get consumers interested in it. It's a well-worn *Quaff* notion that if something is unfashionable, it is likely to represent much better value than something that is trendy.

The reliables –
consistent-quality wines, year in, year out

Still the nation's most consistent cabernet sauvignon at this price point is the popular Lindemans 'Bin 45', which has appeared in five out of six editions of *Quaff*.

Buying and Drinking Cabernet Sauvignon – Some Tips

Short-term cellaring

Most cabernets made at this price point are designed to be approachable so that they can be consumed young. As a general rule, if they are priced below $10 they won't drink any better than they will when you buy them. They should be drunk within six months or so – although they may last perfectly well for longer. If they are priced above $10, they may well benefit from short-term cellaring (six months to a year or two) as they are likely to mellow a bit and become an even better drink. If you are going to cellar some wine, store it in the coolest, darkest room you can find – ideally one without much temperature variation. You'll find that the better the storage conditions, the longer you can keep the wine.

Cabernet sauvignon and food

I generally drink wine with food. If I were to be drinking a red wine at a party or in some situation without food, I would avoid cabernet sauvignon. I'd be looking for something much gentler. With food, however, it's a different matter. Cabernet can be transformed by food. It appears much softer, more supple, even more mellow – those tannins appear to be gulped up by the wine. Best matches include full-flavoured meat dishes – steak, roast lamb, venison or kangaroo fillets, especially served with robust sauces – and hard cheeses such as parmesan or cheddar. Appropriate matches can include casseroles such as lamb shanks, osso buco or coq au vin – especially if you can slip a bit of the wine into the dish.

▰ BLOODY GOOD

2002 Jamiesons Run Cabernet Sauvignon $14

This is an attractive Coonawarra cabernet made by Andrew Hales, who has been doing great things for Beringer Blass in recent years. It has perfumed vanillin oak, intense cassis and dark plum flavours, a pleasing juiciness and nice balance. Some may feel that there's a bit too much oak but, for me, the wine has enough depth of fruit to stand up to that. Perfect with hearty braised lamb shanks.

2004 Roberts Estate Cabernet Sauvignon $10

Roberts Estate is a large winery based at Merbein in the Murray–Darling, which has come up trumps with a wine like this. It has some floral notes on the nose, is clean, fresh, vibrant and juicy with red jube and raspberry flavours. Delicious, easy-drinking.

2003 Wolf Blass 'Yellow Label' Cabernet Sauvignon $14.95

This is the top label of Wolf Blass at the *Quaff* price point and shows the experience of the company and the resources available to them. It's vibrant and juicy, has attractive redcurrant flavours, and impeccable balance between fruit and oak.

▰ GOOD

2004 Angus the Bull Cabernet Sauvignon $14

Hamish McGowan's concept is simple: each vintage make one red that is designed to be drunk with prime beef and market it under this clever label. McGowan sources it from around Australia – usually with a fair contribution of fruit from the Barossa and McLaren Vale. It's been a huge hit, especially in the USA. This is a delight: light- to medium-bodied, soft, round and smooth with ripe cassis and redcurrant flavours and finishing with strong acidity.

2003 De Bortoli 'Deen Vat 9' Cabernet Sauvignon $9

This is what they call a 'crowd pleaser'. Which means it won't please everybody. It's a big red: dense, black berry and dark plum flavours, voluminous vanillin oak, a firm structure and quite heavy, though ripe, tannins. If you love huge oaky wines, you'll love this. There are plenty of more elegant, finer wines for you to choose in this chapter if your tastes are otherwise.

2004 Lindemans 'Bin 45' Cabernet Sauvignon $8.95

A well-made quaffer featuring vibrant, ripe, sweet fruit, reasonable weight, almost fleshy texture, and good balance. Great price.

2004 Queen Adelaide Cabernet Sauvignon $7.45

A lively, light-bodied cabernet that is juicy and has sweet red berry fruit. Unpretentious but easy to enjoy.

2004 Rouge Homme Cabernet Sauvignon $14.95

This has some of the richness and concentration of flavour that you'd expect from a bright, young Coonawarra cabernet. While it could be argued that it lacks the finesse, elegance or depth of the best of the breed, it is flavoursome, approachable and reasonably priced.

2003 Scarpantoni 'Pedler Creek' Cabernet Sauvignon $14

A quaffer from McLaren Vale's Scarpantoni, which needed a bit of a swirl to clean it up at first – that can happen when a wine is under screwcap. This is a nicely balanced varietal with smooth texture, ripe plummy, dark berry flavours and a fine, gentle finish.

2004 Tobacco Road Cabernet Sauvignon $11

This King Valley cabernet is dominated by its American oak treatment, so you'll find heaps of vanillin (almost coconut-flavoured) oak, some dark berry flavours and a clean, supple finish. This has appeal if you like oak.

2004 Tyrrells 'Lost Block' Cabernet Sauvignon $13.95

Sourced from McLaren Vale, this unoaked style has quite complex flavours – mulberry, brambles and tamarillo – and is lively, fresh and juicy.

▰ PRETTY GOOD

2003 Deakin Estate Cabernet Sauvignon $10

In 2003, as in most vintages, this consistent cabernet is soft, round and ripe – made for relaxed drinking.

2003 Houghton Cabernet Sauvignon $12

I don't remember the Houghton Cabernet having so much charry oak and dense vanilla characters as in this vintage. It does, however, have reasonable depth of dark berry fruit and power.

2003 Kingston Estate Cabernet Sauvignon $13

Lots of clean, bright fruit in balance with gentle oak, just a bit bitter on the finish for me. You could mask that with a rib-eye steak and some home-cut chips.

2004 McPherson Cabernet Sauvignon $8.95

This large Goulburn Valley winery has produced an oaky red with cassis and redcurrant flavours and a touch of sweetness to soften its firm, grippy finish.

2001 Morris Cabernet Sauvignon $14.95

A clean, lively cabernet with redcurrant and red cherry flavours.

2004 Red Deer Station Cabernet Sauvignon $12.95

From a second label of the Riverina's Dal Broi comes this light-bodied red with sweet redcurrant fruit and strong acidity on the finish.

2004 Wyndham Estate 'Bin 444' Cabernet Sauvignon $13.95

Substantial red with plenty of cedary oak, powerful fruit and firm, ripe tannins.

MERLOT

As a general rule, merlot probably deserved the bashing it received in the film *Sideways* when Miles declared 'I'm leaving if anyone orders merlot'. As a varietal in Australia, too often it is thin, green, weedy, over-oaked and completely lacking in charm. At its rare best – when it is ripe, silkily textured, in harmony with its gentle oak – it can be immediately appealing and a great drink. But merlot doesn't have to be expensive to be good. Just look at the Bloody Good and Good wines in this chapter.

Although the film *Sideways* did boost sales of pinot noir and cause a decline in the popularity of merlot in the USA, I doubt that it has had the same impact in Australia. Certainly, the amount of merlot harvested in Australia in 2005 increased by more than either of its closest red wine rivals. Merlot rose by 16 per cent (to 144,400 tonnes) while shiraz crept up 4 per cent (to 454,200 tonnes) and cabernet declined by 5 per cent (to 303,600 tonnes). To put this in perspective, 1000 tonnes were produced in 1988 and 8000 tonnes in 1996.

While plenty of expensive merlots disappoint, there are many very drinkable merlots at the quaffing price points. In fact, it seems that when the winemakers chill-out and don't try too hard to cram too much oak into the wine or extract every last ounce of tannin, the result can be much more drinkable – a fun-filled, juicy red fruit bomb that is a pleasure to gulp. Don't doubt it for a second: merlot is still popular, especially in quaffland.

The reliables –
consistent-quality wines, year in, year out

Two merlots have appeared in five out of six editions of *Quaff*, making them consistent and reliable examples of the variety: Rosemount Estate and McWilliams Hanwood.

Buying and Drinking Merlot – Some Tips

Balance is all

You'll see very clearly the style of merlot that I believe makes the best drink: those that don't have too much oak or tannins, which are over-extractive, and those that aren't too heavy or too strong. This means that the wines need to be balanced – the fruit should match the oak treatment and the tannins. As a general rule, wines at this price point have neither the richness nor the concentration to cope with a great deal of oak or massive tannins. That's why merlot is often at its best when it's least manipulated.

Different styles

Having stated a clear preference for soft, smooth, easy-drinking and fleshy merlots (especially at the *Quaff* price point), it should be said that I also admire the bigger, bolder, more robust and savoury reds, which have a dry, tannic grip: wines such as the Yalumba, the Conti 'Medici Ridge', the Peter Lehmann and the Sticks. These are different in style but avoid excessive oaking and heavy tannins.

BLOODY GOOD

2004 Beresford 'Highwood' Merlot $13

The best of McLaren Vale's Beresford in this year's *Quaff* is this nicely balanced merlot – oak held in check, tannin not aggressive, softer and fleshier than most with red berry and plum flavours. Approachable, drinkable: *Quaff* on!

2004 McWilliams 'Hanwood' Merlot $12

Nothing indicates more clearly why the Hanwood range have been so successful for McWilliams – at home and abroad – than this delicious merlot. It has attractive macerated cherry characters, some vanillin oak showing off the sweet fruit, some fleshy texture and a fresh, clean, lively finish. Oak and tannins held neatly in check. Pleasant, approachable, easy to like.

2004 Penfolds 'Rawsons Retreat' Merlot $10.95

Another merlot that hits the mark by leaving the grapes to express themselves without overwhelming them with oak or tannins. Restrained on the nose, but soft and fleshy texture, bright, almost bouncy, redcurrant, jubes, and juicy plum flavours are followed by a lovely gentle finish. Value.

2003 Taylors Merlot $17

This appears to be discounted below $15 regularly enough to justify it being one of the very few wines with a recommended retail price above $15 that I've slotted into this section of *Quaff*. The Clare Valley's largest producer has been a favourite of *Quaff* and is, unquestionably, one of the Australian wineries that most consistently delivers excellent value to its consumers. I much preferred the 2003 merlot – with its velvety texture, sweet, ripe red berry flavours and rich, fleshy finish – to the 2004, which I find more sturdy and less sumptuous (or do I mean 'seductive'?).

2003 Yalumba 'Y Series' Merlot $11.95

In *Quaff 2005* we commented that this red was a dark, oaky, gutsy expression of the variety and unlike previous vintages. Tasting it again for this year's book showed that the 2003 Yalumba Merlot had benefited enormously from an additional six months in the bottle. It is still quite big and brooding with heaps of power but is softer and smoother and the oak is much better integrated than before. Ripe dark plum flavours before a spicy sweet vanillin finish. Value.

 GOOD

2002 Logan 'Weemala' Merlot $14.95

The wines from the Logan family just keep on getting better and better. While the images of local birds on the label are striking, I find the name 'Weemala', an Aboriginal word for 'good view', cumbersome and suspect that consumers might find it difficult to remember. This 2002 Merlot – labelled Central Ranges as it's from Orange and Mudgee – is neatly focused, strictly varietal (redcurrant and plum flavours), and has attractive, silky texture and well-balanced oak.

2004 Paul Conti 'Medici Ridge' Merlot $14

Sourced from the Conti family's Manjimup vineyard, among the tall timbers of Western Australia's south-west, this is a robust merlot with powerful vanillin oak flavours, ripe fruit, fleshy texture and full-on tannins. It's approachable now, especially with an equally robust osso buco or the like.

2003 Peter Lehmann Merlot $14.95

The 2005 *Quaff* Winery of the Year continues its good work with wines like this lively little number. OK, so this is the Barossa and so expect some tannin and oak. However, it's made by Andrew Wigan and the Lehmann team so it's nicely balanced. Smooth, fleshy, ripe flavours.

2004 Red Deer Station Merlot $12.95

This is another of the labels developed by the Griffith-based Dal Broi family from the 1800 hectares that it has under vines. The unoaked merlot is soft, round and fleshy, has ripe plummy flavours and some firmness on the finish.

2004 Sandalford 'Element' Merlot $12

Winemaker Paul Boulden continues to lift the bar for this major Western Australian producer at all price points. This is the third vintage of a red that is sourced from old vines on the company's Swan Valley vineyard (52 per cent), its mature Wilyabrup vineyard (23 per cent) and growers in the south-west. There's heaps of softness, deep red berry flavours and a gentle, balanced finish.

2003 Scarpantoni 'Pedler Creek' Merlot $14

A McLaren Vale producer that is getting – and earning – more attention recently. This has the seductiveness that you'd expect from the region's warm climate: fleshy, ripe, weighty, full-flavoured with only moderate tannins.

2003 Sticks Yarra Valley Merlot $14.95

Rated Bloody Good in last year's *Quaff* and still available in bottleshop land (that shows how tough the market is at present), Rob Dolan's Sticks Merlot was described as a 'lovely, pure, way-too-good-to-be-under-$15, juicy, medium-bodied red. Very sophisticated wine for the price.' While it lacks the vibrance that it showed 12 months ago, it's still a classy expression of the variety.

2004 Zilzie Merlot $14.95

The Forbes family have been farming the land at Karadoc, not far from Mildura, since 1911. Not content to supply grapes to Southcorp from their huge 250 hectare vineyard, they added winemaking to their repertoire in 2000 with a good deal of success. This merlot is soft, round and ripe with sweet red berry fruit, a lovely smoothness and fine, gentle finish.

▄▶ PRETTY GOOD

2004 Evans & Tate 'Gnangara' Merlot $13.95

There's plenty of ripeness and softness from this West Aussie merlot along with cedary oak and a firmish finish. Try it at the sausage sizzle.

2004 Lindemans 'Bin 40' Merlot $9

Light-bodied and consistent to this style, softer than many and pleasantly straightforward.

2004 Lindemans 'Cawarra' Merlot $6.95

This vintage of the 'Cawarra' merlot was rated Bloody Good last year – for its generous plummy fruit and richness that 'works well as an example of a bouncy young merlot'. It's lost its bounce and seems much more tannic than before. Pretty good for the price but unless you've become addicted to it, I'd wait for the next vintage.

2003 Palandri 'Baldivis' Merlot $11.95

There some earthy, gamey characters and sweet fruit, reasonably smooth texture and restrained tannins to finish.

2004 Queen Adelaide Merlot $7.45

Modestly priced, light-bodied red with intense dark berry fruit, richness in the mid-palate and lively tannins.

2003 Redbank 'Long Paddock' Merlot $12

> Sourced from growers in the King and Ovens Valleys, this has ripe plummy flavours, fleshy texture and a soft, gentle finish.

2003 Roberts Estate Merlot $9.95

> Roberts Estate is based at Merbein in the Murray–Darling and is a major processor of grapes. This is soft, plummy and easy-drinking except for a touch oaky and tannic on the finish.

2002 Rosemount Estate 'Diamond Label' Merlot $14.95

> A soft, round, pleasant easy-drinking merlot with some redcurrant flavours, plummy fruitcake and a gentle finish.

2003 Sarantos Merlot $12.95

> Another label of Kingston Estate that features a sturdy powerful red with dark plum flavours, smooth texture and yet is neither excessively oaky nor tannic.

2003 Tall Poppy Merlot $13.95

> Another Murray–Darling producer from close to marvellous Mildura (think Stefano di Pieri and all that superb food) – ripe redcurrant flavours, smooth enough texture, just a bit too much oak.

SHIRAZ

While shiraz remains as popular as ever and demand for merlot continues to grow, cabernet sauvignon has become a hard sell and the current glut hits most solidly at those grape growers who produce cabernet. Stories abound of growers leaving tonnes of cabernet on the grapes because they don't consider picking it worthwhile. Although I believe that stories of cabernet's demise are exaggerated, there is no doubting which is the red variety that locals and our export markets are clamouring for most loudly.

Shiraz had a 43% increase in 2004 and a modest 4% increase in 2005 to 454,000 tonnes. In 1996, it was only 80,000 tonnes so the increase in the past decade has been phenomenal. Putting that in perspective total production of wine since 1994 has grown by 180% while the increase in Australian exports has been 350%.

As it usually does, shiraz makes up the largest section in this book, with more than a hundred wines tasted. More shiraz are recommended than ever before although still less than 10% of wines tasted receive the Bloody Good rating. Those include some of the standout bargains in the book.

The reliables –
consistent-quality wines, year in, year out

Rosemount Estate 'Diamond Label' is the only shiraz to be found in all six editions of *Quaff*. Amazingly for a wine at its price, it won two trophies against much more expensive opposition at the 2004 Cowra Show.

Buying and Drinking Shiraz – Some Tips

Gluggability

Most people buy a bottle of wine and drink it for dinner that night. They are looking for an immediately appealing wine that they can consume with confidence. For a mid-week quaffing red, it's hard to beat a bright spicy Aussie shiraz from the Riverina, Murray-Darling or Riverland – that sells for less than $10 a bottle. With their light-body and vibrant fruity flavours, the best of them are great glugging wines.

Betting each way

Shiraz can, of course, be a more substantial drink for much more serious occasions – even at quaffing price points. Many of the medium to full-bodied reds that sell in the $12 to $15 range come either from, or contain a significant proportion of fruit grown in, premium areas such as Coonawarra, Clare, Langhorne Creek or McLaren Vale. These more robust reds are made to be approachable but can often be cellared in the short term – for say one to three years. If you do drink them immediately, make sure you serve them with hearty meat dish (beef casseroles, lamb roast with powerfully flavoured gravy, homemade hamburgers or steak sandwiches). In this chapter, those which are likely to benefit most from aging include the Beelgara 'Silky Oak', Hardys Oomoo, Jamiesons Run, Stepping Stone, and Yalumba Galway.

 BLOODY GOOD

 2003 Beelgara 'Silky Oak' Shiraz $8

THE QUAFF 2006 'Sausages and Chips'
BEST RED WINE UNDER $10 AWARD

This is much more robust than most Riverina reds. You may need to decant this or give it a vigorous swirl before you taste – just to give it some air. It has plummy flavours, fleshy texture, reasonable integration of fruit and oak and firm, prominent tannins to finish. You'd forgive it for that especially if you served it with a hearty sirloin and a lusty, wine-based sauce.

2004 Cheviot Bridge 'CB' Heathcote Shiraz $12.95

This Victorian virtual winery is run by an experienced team of industry personnel – most of whom were associated with Mildara Blass in their former lives. Its export thrust was speeded up by the acquisition of the Long Flat brand from Tyrrells. They are a consistent performer in the value-for-money stakes with wines under the Long Flat, Long Flat Wine Company, CB and Cheviot Bridge labels. This must be, by a long way, the cheapest Heathcote shiraz on the market and it's a terrific red for the price. There is lifted spicy oak, deep redcurrant, dark plum (and even Christmas cake) flavours and a smooth, fleshy texture. It's ripe, even overripe, and a bit hot (spirited) on the finish. Still, it's approachable now and will improve over the next year or two. Bargain.

2002 Fox River Shiraz $14.95

I liked this when I first tasted it last January and was once again impressed when I saw it as part of my tastings for *Quaff 2006*. It's the Goundrey second label, which has performed well in *Quaff* over the past few years – sometimes, indeed, better than the winery's main label. However, there have been some encouraging signs that Goundrey is getting back on song. And this wine indicates that the Fox River label is as good as ever. There is some alluring white pepper on the nose showing the wine's cool climate origins; the palate is smooth and succulent; and there's more of that spicy, white pepper flavour lingering on the finish.

2003 Hardys 'Oomoo' Shiraz $13.95

A favourite of mine, the 2005 *Quaff* Red Wine of the Year, and the best of the three vintages so far released under this wonderfully old-fashioned label. It has all the rich textures and lavish flavours that we've come to expect of McLaren Vale shiraz. Approachable and still with years of life.

2002 Jacobs Creek Reserve Shiraz $15.95

Hard to believe that a wine as good as this from the brilliant 2002 vintage is still around. Soft and round with rich, concentrated red berry flavours, good weight and ripe, moderate tannins. Drinking well.

2003 Rosemount Estate 'Diamond Label' Shiraz $14.95

Winning two trophies in open company at the Cowra Show is an amazing feat for a wine at this price point. This was reviewed in last year's *Quaff* thus: 'There are no surprises with this old favourite: it is succulent, medium-bodied, with redcurrant and dark plum flavours, supple texture and a fair tannin whack to finish. As ever, it's a good drink.' It's still available, which is surprising for a double trophy winner. I must say that I still find the tannins pretty heavy and the texture chewy so, although it's a well-performed wine, I don't enjoy it all that much.

2002 Stonehaven 'Stepping Stone' Shiraz $12.99

I had a great weekend in Padthaway late last year, checking out the wineries and vineyards of the most northerly of the Limestone Coast regions. What impressed me most was the quality of the shiraz from the region. The Stepping Stone was the stand-out of the quaffing reds in a blind line-up at the Harvest Festival: soft, round and full, mulberry, dark plum and spicy oak flavours with some eucalyptus notes and ripe, firm yet well-integrated tannins. A seriously good red from Stonehaven's Sue Bell.

2004 Woop Woop Shiraz $12.95

In an age when battered wine writers are besieged by impossible-to-pronounce, impossible-to-remember new labels, the likes of omnipresent winemaker Ben Riggs and the owner of McLaren Vale's Pennys Hill – Tony Parkinson – come to our rescue with this catchy, impossible to forget new label, Woop Woop. Even more pleasing, the wines are good and very well priced. This shiraz is so approachable – soft, round, balanced with good richness and concentration of cranberry and fruitcake flavours and a fresh, clean finish.

 GOOD

2003 Andrew Garrett Shiraz $14

A generous shiraz from the Beringer Blass stable that has minty, mentholy flavours and quite a firm finish. Try with your favourite bangers and mash.

2003 Cookoothama Shiraz $14.95

From Nugan Estate in the Riverina comes a plush, velvety shiraz that has intense, ripe dark berry flavours, good weight and fine approachable tannins. There is plenty of oak but the fruit stands up to it well.

2004 De Bortoli 'Black Creek' Shiraz $12.95

An impressive light-bodied Riverina shiraz that has smooth texture and reasonably concentrated redcurrant and plum flavours and a gentle finish.

2003 Deakin Estate Shiraz $9.95

Deakin is based at Red Cliffs near Mildura in the Murray–Darling and is a consistent producer of good wines at quaffing prices. This is light-bodied, clean and fresh with strawberry and plum flavours that linger.

2002 Jamiesons Run Shiraz $14.95

I liked this rich, fleshy, densely flavoured shiraz but it does have heaps of oak. If you like the oak, go for it.

2004 Jip Jip Rocks Shiraz $14.95

I would have thought that the Bryson family's Morambro Creek would have been too small for a second label, but here it is! A terrific, well-priced Padthaway shiraz: perfumed vanillin oak, succulent, rich, concentrated and fleshy, and firm and grippy to finish. Approachable.

2003 Lindemans Reserve Shiraz $12.95

Still available from last year. The Lindemans Reserve label consistently offers quality at the right price. Best of all is this shiraz, much of which comes from McLaren Vale and Padthaway: ripe, rich, concentrated and smooth.

2004 Little Penguin Shiraz $10.95

The new US label targeted at Yellow Tail's success and an impressive debut. While there's no finesse here, it is densely flavoured with heaps of charry oak. What the less sophisticated of us might describe as giving plenty of bang for your buck. Sure to appeal in the USA.

2004 McWilliams 'Hanwood' Shiraz $12

The 'Hanwood' label is a consistent performer across the range – over-delivering at its price point. One contributing factor has been the use of a significant volume (about 20 per cent) of Coonawarra fruit. This is delightfully perfumed, vibrant and balanced with sweet red berry fruit and a touch of oak.

2003 Mitchelton 'Preece' Shiraz $14.95

I liked the wine for its concentration of flavour, smooth texture, juiciness and approachability, though some may find it a bit oaky and grippy to finish. With a robust osso buco this will be less noticeable.

2003 Saltram 'Makers Table' Shiraz $10

Written up and rated as Good in last year's *Quaff* but rebadged under this awful 'Makers Table' label: still with dense, black fruit flavours, smooth texture and ripe approachable tannins.

2003 Saltram 'Next Chapter' Shiraz $14.95

I'd prefer the cheaper of the two Saltram shiraz. This is quite sturdy and oaky with black pepper and bright fruit flavours: a good drink.

2004 Terra Felix Shiraz Viognier $14.95

Perhaps the country's cheapest shiraz viognier – from this popular second label of Tallarook in Central Victoria. It has good depth of clean, fresh, bright fruit, is neatly balanced and is very easy to drink.

2004 Westend Estate 'Outback' Shiraz $7.95

Trophy winner at the 2005 Burswood Perth Show as Best Early Drinking Dry Red. Delightful, easy-drinking style – straightforward with ripe, plummy fruit and fresh lively tannins.

2003 Wolf Blass 'Yellow Label' Shiraz $14

There's something comforting when another vintage of an old favourite comes up trumps: everything is in its place and all's well with the world. So it was this week with tastings for the 2006 edition of *Quaff* in full swing and 50 young shiraz needing to be subjected to rigorous examination. To give a sense of perspective, I wasn't all that impressed with the Wolf Blass 'Eaglehawk' Shiraz – a few dollars cheaper but not in the same class as the Yellow Label red. This is big, robust and has dense, red berry and black plum flavours with heaps of vanillin oak and substantial tannins to finish. Still, the fruit has power and depth and so stands up perfectly well to the oak treatment. There's vibrance, fleshiness and a satisfying approachability about the wine. Fair price too.

▶ PRETTY GOOD

2003 Angove's 'Red Belly Black' Shiraz $14

Powerful, vanillin oak flavours dominate.

2003 Beelgara Estate '15.03' Black Shiraz $14.95

A good quaffer for those who enjoy their wines on the oaky side.

2003 De Bortoli 'Deen Vat 8' Shiraz $9.95

Rich and concentrated, yet firm and oaky.

2003 Haselgrove Shiraz $10

A fresh, lively quaffer that is fair value for the money.

2002 Jacobs Creek Shiraz $9.95

A straightforward and pleasant quaffing red that is clean and well-made.

2004 Queen Adelaide Shiraz $7.45

A clean, fresh light-bodied red with macerated cherry flavours.

2004 Red Deer Station Unoaked Shiraz $12.95

From the Riverina's Dal Broi comes this smooth ripe plummy red that is good current drinking.

2003 Roberts Estate Shiraz $9.95
2004 Roberts Estate Shiraz $9.95

Both vintages are drinking well with my preference for the younger wine: medium-bodied, ripe, sweet red berry flavours.

2003 Tall Poppy 'Select' Shiraz $7.95

Sourced from the Murray–Darling, near Mildura, this is the cheaper of the two Tall Poppy shiraz, and my preferred wine. It's fragrant and fresh with good balance between the dark berry fruit and vanillin oak.

2002 Tall Poppy Shiraz $13.95

> This needed a swirl to clean it up but it was fine thereafter: soft, balanced with attractive red berry flavours.

2002 Trentham Estate Shiraz $14

> Easy drinking with plenty of coconutty oak and savoury dark fruit flavours.

2004 Westend Estate 'Richland' Shiraz $11

> Fresh blackberry and dark plum flavours, lively with smooth texture.

2003 Yalumba 'Galway Vintage' Shiraz $12.95

> Rich and concentrated flavours but the finish is very tannic.

2003 Yellow Tail Shiraz $9.95

> Attractive creamy oak, macerated red plum flavours, firm to finish but still approachable.

OTHER RED VARIETALS

Think about the reds in this chapter as including a group of grapes that have been around in Australia for some time – malbec, pinot noir, petit verdot as well as tarrango and chambourcin – and some classic European varieties that are beginning to be planted in significant amounts – barbera, sangiovese and tempranillo. It's a pretty diverse bunch.

There is some excitement with the best of these wines. Many provide taste experiences outside the mainstream and are recommended for much the same reason as I'd advocate trying some exotic varieties that have been imported from overseas: being adventurous can be fun.

The reliables –
consistent-quality wines, year in, year out

The wonderfully robust Bleasdale Malbec is one of the reliables and has been included in every edition of *Quaff*. The Rosemount Estate Pinot Noir is another favourite, while labels that have consistently appeared in this chapter include De Bortoli 'Windy Peak' and Zilzie.

Buying and Drinking Other Red Varieties – Some Tips

The perfect match
Thinking about what wines will go best with what foods should probably start with traditional matches. Duck and pinot noir are considered a classic pairing, although I believe that lighter-bodied meats such as veal and pork will also work well – especially when the dish incorporates mushrooms, which find an earthy echo in the wine. Sangiovese will go well with many Tuscan dishes and also try roast pork, pasta with tomato-based pasta dishes, or even pizza. More full-bodied reds such as malbec and petit verdot demand robust, slow-cooked meat dishes or grilled steak with hearty red-wine sauces.

Wines by the glass
Look for the opportunity to try these varieties in restaurants and cafes, especially when you can experiment by buying by the glass. When you find a variety you like, look around for a few more examples that suit your palate and add that variety to your vinous portfolio.

▬► BLOODY GOOD

2002 Bleasdale Malbec $13.50

This robust red from Langhorne Creek is one of the reliables that has appeared in each edition of *Quaff*. Surprisingly, the 2002 is the same vintage that was reviewed last year: I would have expected it to have been snapped up by now. It's a substantial, lavishly flavoured malbec with rich, concentrated dark berry flavours, heaps of spicy oak, yet is smooth and well-balanced.

2004 De Bortoli 'Windy Peak' Sangiovese $12.95

The 2002 'Windy Peak' Sangiovese was lovely, the 2003 was delicious and, already, the 2004 is out and it's just soooo scrummy and bold and gluggable that I'm tempted to say it's the best yet. Traditionalists might be a bit cranky that this new vintage isn't 'authentic' enough – ie, it isn't as savoury and dry and 'serious' as sangiovese from Italy – and I can see their point; it certainly doesn't have the same raspy finish that made the 2003 much more distinctively 'varietal'. But it has such a great volume of sangiovese's other great asset – dark, black sour cherry fruit-juiciness – that I'm prepared to overlook its lack of 'authenticity' and focus instead on its drinkability.

2004 Long Flat Wine Company Pinot Noir $13.95

The key thing about pinot noir is that it must have the fragrance and texture that is typical of the variety. That is rare in wines in this segment of the market. The Long Flat has raspberry jube and spicy strawberry flavours, is soft, round and silky, with a gentle finish of some length.

2004 Sticks Pinot Noir $14.95

This is a stand-out pinot, which shows the quality that is possible from the variety in the Yarra Valley. Most importantly, it has very good varietal character, is delicate yet intense, has strawberry and raspberry flavours, a lovely mouthfeel and fine, soft finish. Brilliant value for money.

2004 Zilzie Sangiovese $14.95

These guys from Karadoc in the Murray–Darling are impressing with their handling of exotic varieties. This has a wonderful floral nose, spicy tomato bush flavours and the vibrance to make a smart companion to dishes ranging from spaghetti with a Bolognese ragu to veal scaloppine with a marsala sauce.

 GOOD

2004 Angoves 'Stonegate' Petit Verdot' $7.95

A surprise packet from the Riverland: fragrant with powerful deep dark berry flavours and firm, grippy tannins. At its best with a sirloin steak accompanied by a robust red-wine sauce.

2004 Australian Old Vine 'Sovereign Wine' Chambourcin $12

Although this Riverina vineyard has some old vines, the chambourcin doesn't come from those and is released under the 'Sovereign Wine' label. It's all a bit confusing. I'm not the greatest fan of chambourcin but I was impressed by this wine. Thank goodness for blind tastings. There are tamarillo and redcurrant flavours, silky texture, good weight and a pleasing grip to finish.

2004 Barrecas Barbera $15

A favourite of mine from a tiny Donnybrook winery (in the Geographe region of Western Australia) owned by the Barrecas family and driven by twenty-somethings Fil (who does the viticulture) and Iolanda (who crafts the wine). It's made with creamy, toasty oak and high alcohol. It is powerful, robust, fleshy and drinks well young. Mainly cellar door.

2003 Cape Schanck Pinot Noir $14.95

This is a second label from the Mornington producer T'Gallant, owned by Beringer Blass. It is easy to drink, with strawberry and redcurrant flavours, smooth texture and a gentle, if slightly hot, finish.

2004 Tall Poppy 'Hillside' Petit Verdot $9.95

Most petit verdots from warm regions such as the Murray–Darling have deep, dark berry flavours and powerful full-bodied structure. This is more light-bodied with lively juicy red berry flavours (redcurrant and raspberry) and noticeable acidity to finish.

2004 Zilzie Petit Verdot $14.95

Zilzie and Tall Poppy are both based near Mildura. Their petit verdots could not be more different. The Zilzie is more typical of the style: inky dark with vibrant briary, brambly flavours, smooth, almost velvety, texture and a bold tannic finish.

2004 Zilzie Tempranillo $14.95

Zilzie continues the form that it showed last year with this classic Spanish variety, which is proving a hit when sourced from Australia's warmer wine regions. This has good weight, smooth, almost silky, texture, wild cherry and savoury dark berry flavours, and tannins that grip, yet remain approachable.

▶ PRETTY GOOD

2004 Brown Brothers Tarrango $12

> This hybrid, especially bred for warm regions, is a consistent crowd-pleaser for Brown Brothers: lively, light redcurrant flavours.

2003 'Mr Frog' Pinot Noir $14.95

> Pleasant, gentle and juicy. Could do with more varietal character, but drinks well.

2004 Rosemount Estate 'Diamond Label' Pinot Noir $14.95

> Over the past six years, this has been the most consistently good pinot noir under $15 in the country. Soft, pleasant, flavoursome.

2004 Scarpantoni 'Pedler Creek' Sangiovese $14

> A fragrant quaffer with decent red cherry flavours and very powerful tannins to finish.

2004 Tempus Two Tempranillo $13.95

> The texture here is interestingly different: thick, viscous, almost syrupy. Full-flavoured and savoury.

CABERNET MERLOT BLENDS

The number of wines tasted in this category is slightly up on last year and has increased significantly since the first edition of *Quaff*. In spite of the temporary glitch caused by the bashing merlot received in the film *Sideways*, its popularity continues undiminished in Australia. Because of the huge amount of merlot planted in the last decade, there are significantly more varietal merlots and heaps available for cabernet merlot blends. The ease of pronunciation and the mellifluous sound of the word 'merlot' has surely helped its popularity, as has its perceived softness.

The marriage of cabernet sauvignon – with its firmer structure, occasionally hollow mid-palate and drying grip – and merlot – with its fleshy smoothness, plump mid-palate and softer, gentler finish can produce some beautifully balanced, flavoursome reds. But the reality is that only six out of more than 50 cabernet merlots have been rated Bloody Good. Only half of those tasted are reviewed in this chapter. Many of the other wines are either powerful, oaky and almost unapproachable, or skinny and tough.

The reliables –
consistent-quality wines, year in, year out

This is an emerging category with no clear-cut reliables. Most consistent have been Andrew Garrett, Lindemans, Rouge Homme, Rosemount Estate, Saltram and Trentham Estate.

Buying and Drinking Cabernet Merlot Blends – Some Tips

The $10 price point

There tends to be a division between those wines under $10 and those which sell for between $10 and $15. The best of the former have more redcurrant, raspberry flavours while the latter tend to have darker berry fruit – often because of the addition of up to 20 per cent of fruit from some of Australia's premium regions. Those under $10 usually come from regions along the Murray River (the Riverland, Swan Hill and Murray–Darling) and the Murrumbidgee (the Riverina). They are lighter-bodied and more straightforward, but the best of them are delicious, everyday quaffers.

Bottle age

A number of those cabernet merlots that have been recommended come from premium regions and have enough richness and concentration of flavour and sufficient tannin grip to improve with time in your cellar. Rolling, Andrew Garrett and Lindemans Reserve are the most likely to benefit from additional bottle age. Having said that, the great thing about under-$15 wines is that they are approachable enough to drink now without having to worry about cellaring.

🍷 BLOODY GOOD

2003 Andrew Garrett Cabernet Merlot $14

This is one of the Beringer Blass quaffing labels to look out for. The 2003 is much better than the previous vintage of the wine: creamy cedary oak, smooth as silk, rich and concentrated with ripe plummy flavours. Drinking beautifully.

2004 Broken Earth Cabernet Merlot $9.95

Tandou, a huge operation with more than 1450 hectares of vineyards in two locations in the Murray–Darling, releases wines under the Broken Earth and Wontanella labels. This is a big, bold, robust red with concentrated blackcurrant, dark plum and charry oak flavours and smooth – almost velvety – texture. There is heaps of oak but the fruit has enough depth to carry it. Not for the faint-hearted – my wife, Elaine, would love it – but impressive, especially at the price.

2004 De Bortoli 'Sacred Hill' Cabernet Merlot $6–$8

At the 2005 Sydney Show, the Riverina producer De Bortoli won two trophies. Its 2002 Noble One ($44 for a 750 ml bottle) won the trophy for best sweet wine of the show. No surprise there. It's arguably been Australia's top sticky since it was first released in 1982. De Bortoli also won the Australian Wine and Brandy Corporation Trophy for the best red wine with a retail value under $20 for its 2004 De Bortoli 'Sacred Hill' Cabernet Merlot – which sells for $8 (or less). De Bortoli have been one of the stars of *Quaff* and each year they seem to come up with at least one remarkable red that sells for less than $10. Their slightly more expensive quaffers in the Windy Peak and Gulf Station ranges offer consistent value at quaffing prices. Under $10, we need to search around. Last year, our favourite was the 2003 De Bortoli Wild Vine Shiraz – *Quaff*'s Best Red Under $10. A few year before that the 2001 Sacred Hill Cabernet Merlot was sensational. My theory, based on observation over the past six years, is that while not every De Bortoli red under $10 will be brilliant, there is likely to be at least one red in their portfolio that is stunning for the price. This year, it's the 2004 'Sacred Hill' Cabernet Merlot: soft and round, clean, fresh and lively, ripe, plummy, uncomplicated flavours. Delicious quaffing.

2002 Lindemans Reserve Cabernet Merlot $12.95

Last year, the 2003 was featured in *Quaff* and now we are back to the 2002 vintage. This is sourced from the Limestone Coast with most of the fruit coming from Southcorp's vineyard in Bordertown. It's a pretty oaky style – even though Lindemans only use two- and three-year-old barrels. Still, it's approachable with the added bonus of some delightful succulence, has good weight, bright dark berry flavours with vanilla bean and mocha and soft, ripe tannins.

2004 Queen Adelaide Cabernet Merlot $7.45

Those sun-drenched vineyards along the Murray rarely provide us with more delightful quaffing wines than this. It's packed with enough vibrant squishy, juicy, ripe raspberry jube and redcurrant flavours to satisfy those of us who lust after flavour. No rough edges for the critics to carp about. Just a satisfying quaffer! Promoted to Bloody Good because of its bargain basement price.

2003 Cumulus 'Rolling' Cabernet Merlot $14

I fell in love with Orange after a whirlwind day zipping around the region with winemaker Philip Shaw (OK, it's always a whirlwind day with Philip Shaw) late last year. It really is a picture-postcard perfect place. The landscape features gentle undulating slopes still all shades of green in December, precisely laid out vines, hectares of apple orchards while the local cherries were just coming into season. The 2003 Rolling Cabernet Merlot comes from the 508 hectare Cumulus vineyard, which is being pulled back by the viticultural team so that its yields are significantly reduced. It has ripe plummy, black cherry flavours, soft, silky smooth texture and fine, gentle tannins. Delicious.

◗ GOOD

2003 Cheviot Bridge 'CB' Cabernet Merlot $12.95

While it may need a swirl or two of the glass at first, or some time in a decanter, this is a pleasant, robust red with ripe redcurrant and plum flavours and gentle, ripe tannins.

2004 Evans & Tate 'Salisbury' Cabernet Merlot $9.95

The best wine we saw in the *Quaff* tastings from Evans & Tate's Mildura operation: soft, round, redcurrant and raspberry flavours, clean, fresh, almost succulent, finish. Easy-drinking.

2003 Ferngrove Cabernet Merlot $14.95

Kim Horton, Vanessa Carson and the Ferngrove team at Frankland River have made a delightful quaffer from the 2003 vintage: smooth, ripe, redcurrant and plum flavours, relatively light-bodied for the region but a better quaffer for that.

2002 Kirrihill Estates 'Companions' Cabernet Merlot $12.95

A very good cheapie from the Clare Valley – intense black fruit flavours, heaps of vanillin oak, lovely juiciness. Perfect with sausages, onions, mash and a robust gravy.

2004 Lindemans 'Cawarra' Cabernet Merlot $6.95

There are several impressive performances from this entry-level label of Lindemans in this year's *Quaff*. It has gentle cedary oak, fleshy texture, ripe red berry fruit, and is attractive drinking. At the price, it's worth the Good ranking.

2004 Rosemount Estate 'Diamond Label' Cabernet Merlot $10.95

There's plenty of cedary oak here but it has the bright red berry fruit to match – so it's a pleasant, easy-drinking style, which is juicy, lively and flavoursome with fine, ripe tannins.

2003 Trentham Estate Cabernet Merlot $14.50

> Tony Murphy and his team at the family winery on the lush banks of the Murray just outside Mildura have become firm favourites of *Quaff* because of wines like this. It's a quintessential Aussie red – soft, smooth and easy to drink with heaps of ripe red berry flavours, gentle oak, and a clean, zingy finish. *Quaff* on!

━ PRETTY GOOD

2002 Buckland Gap Cabernet Merlot $9

> A robust little bleeder (oops, I mean 'robust little red') with heaps of coconut-flavoured oak and fleshy texture – for those occasions when substance needs to triumph over style.

2003 Capel Vale CV Cabernet Merlot $15

> A well-made red that is drinking well at present – smooth, rich flavours, pleasant aftertaste.

2004 Cockatoo Ridge Cabernet Merlot $10.25

> An undemanding quaffing red that is smooth, ripe and whooshable.

2003 Coriole '8 Gauge' Cabernet Merlot $14.95

> A clean, well-made McLaren Vale red.

2004 Dal Broi 'Yarranvale Station' Cabernet Merlot $10.95

> It's smooth and velvety with decent flavours and a firm finish. Needs time.

2003 De Bortoli 'Black Creek' Cabernet Merlot $12

> Ripe red berry flavours with a touch of mint, smooth texture. Slips down easily.

2002 Kingston Cabernet Merlot $11.95

> Smooth, easy-drinking red with ripe plummy flavours.

2003 Long Flat Cabernet Merlot $8.95
> A good quaffer at a fair price: ripe red berries with a touch of oak to provide definition.

2004 McWilliams 'Inheritance' Cabernet Merlot $7
> A straightforward barbecue red for those evenings when keeping down the costs is vital.

2004 Rouge Homme Cabernet Merlot $14.95
> A consistent favourite from the Limestone Coast: sweet blackcurrant flavours with a pleasant, grippy finish.

2002 Saltram 'Next Chapter' Cabernet Merlot $14.95
> Robust oaky red with power and concentration of flavour.

2002 Wildfly Cabernet Merlot $14
> From the promising Channybearup vineyards in Pemberton comes a smooth, light-bodied red that has earthy, meat stock and dark plum flavours.

2002 Wyndham Estate 'Bin 888' Cabernet Merlot $13.95
> A lighter style with pleasant flavours and some fine, grippy tannins.

GRENACHE BLENDS

Grenache has been one of Australia's most significant grape varieties because of its suitability in the making of fortifieds – until the last 30 years the most important style of wine produced here. Following the decline in the popularity of fortifieds since the 1970s, grenache was blended away into bulk and cask wines. Yet, as recently as the early 1990s, there was more grenache grown in Australia than cabernet sauvignon. Now there is 12 times as much cabernet as grenache.

What has saved grenache has been the renewed interest in low-yielding, dry-grown old vine grenache in regions such as the Barossa and McLaren Vale and the production of premium, super-premium or ultra-premium grenache from these vineyards. The opulent, powerfully concentrated, ripe, fleshy reds have sold for high prices and helped to forge reputations for the likes of Charles Melton, Torbreck, Clarendon Hills and D'Arenberg.

One of the spin-offs can be seen in the small number of deliciously vibrant quaffers that are represented in this chapter. Especially as part of a blend, grenache can make appealing, gluggable, early drinking reds at affordable prices.

The reliables –
consistent-quality wines, year in, year out
There's been a Peter Lehmann red ever-present in *Quaff*. What was originally marketed as a varietal grenache is now the Shiraz Grenache. This year, they've added a GSM. D'Arenberg 'The Stump Jump' and the Rosemount Estate Grenache Shiraz have been in five out of six editions of *Quaff*.

Buying and Drinking Grenache Blends – Some Tips

A blended red

For the first time in *Quaff*, there are no varietal grenaches in this chapter – just grenache blended with reds, which have an affinity with it. In its homeland, Spain, and in the south of France where it flourishes, grenache (garnacha in Spain) is most often used as part of a red blend.

Young, warm and wonderful

While there are a few exceptions – and they are not at this price point – grenache blends produced in Australia are best consumed young, when they are fresh, fleshy and flavoursome. They are so drinkable that there is no point in cellaring them.

BLOODY GOOD

2004 Heartland 'Stickleback' Red $12

Last year's Best New Label went to Heartland's quaffer, Stickleback. Heartland is owned by a group consisting of Woodstock's Scott Collett, viticulturist Geoff Hardy, Grant Tillbrook and winemaker Ben Glaetzer. The Heartland wines are sourced from the Limestone Coast and are all very well priced. This is a blend of cabernet sauvignon, shiraz and grenache that is rich, ripe and concentrated, has good weight and depth, smooth almost silky texture and a gentle, supple finish. *Quaff* on!

2004 Rosemount Estate Grenache Shiraz $10.95

Very good early-drinking style: soft and round with rich, ripe plum and dark cherry flavours, velvety texture and gentle, balanced finish. The restrained use of oak makes this approachable while the concentration of flavour gives it interest.

2004 Rosemount Estate 'Jigsaw' Shiraz Mataro Grenache $7.95

A delightful cheapie with ripe juicy fruit, brambly, dark berry flavours, smooth texture and a soft, easy-drinking finish. Good summer drinking.

2004 St Hallett 'Gamekeepers' Reserve $14.95

Unquestionably the best vintage of this consistently good Barossa favourite. Stuart Blackwell and St Hallett have made it into four out of the six editions of *Quaff* with the wine. It's a blend of shiraz, grenache, mourvedre and the Portuguese fortified variety, touriga, made for early drinking. The 2004 has the gentle, fleshy texture, which is a signature of the style, but has greater richness, complexity and depth of flavour than any previous vintage of Gamekeepers. It has some briary notes along with redcurrants and mulberry flavours, is smooth and silky, yet has more structure than you'd expect.

 GOOD

2002 Geoff Merrill Shiraz Grenache Mourvedre $14.95

A style that does well in McLaren Vale – ripe red cherry and dark berry flavours, silky texture, good depth and concentration. The vanillin oak is noticeable.

2003 Paul Conti Grenache Shiraz $14.95

From the Swan District region on the outskirts of Perth, where the hard work at this long-established Italian family winery is now done by young(ish) Jason Conti. Subdued on the nose but showing ripe, plummy fruit, reasonable richness and concentration. A good drink.

2003 Peter Lehmann Grenache Shiraz Mourvedre $16

While some might find the oak a touch heavy, most will regard this as a Barossa crowd-pleaser: good concentration of flavour, velvety texture – very easy to drink.

2002 Rosemount Estate Shiraz Grenache Viognier $14.95

> An approachable, easy-drinking young red with fleshy texture, red berry flavours and a gentle grip on the finish.

➤ PRETTY GOOD

2004 Chain of Ponds 'Novello' Nero $14.25

> A blend of sangiovese, grenache and barbera, which makes a significantly different style: denser, heavier, still soft yet chewy, with earthy, gravelly flavours.

2004 Chain of Ponds 'Novello' Rosso $14.25

> Very much in the rosé style, this blend of grenache, mourvedre and sangiovese is soft and approachable, has a savoury edge, and is filled out by sweetness on the finish.

2004 D'Arenberg 'The Stump Jump' Grenache Shiraz Mourvedre $13

> Soft, smooth and flavoursome with pretty strong tannins to finish.

2003 Geoff Merrill 'Liquid Asset' Shiraz Grenache Viognier $14.95

> Straightforward, easy-drinking style from McLaren Vale with decent ripe plummy flavours.

2004 Peter Lehmann Shiraz Grenache $12

> Soft and smooth with raspberry and plum flavours – more oaky and tannic than usual.

SHIRAZ CABERNET BLENDS

The number of wines entered for this chapter is slightly up on last year with some 45 tasted, but the number reviewed is substantially down. A few of those wines have found their way into the over $15 chapter – and are worth checking out. There could be a number of reasons why some of the old favourites haven't made this year's book: because they are no longer made, because they are now sold above the $15 price point, because the new vintage hadn't been released at the time of the tastings or because quality had slipped. Whatever the reason, there'll be some benefits – the weeding out has been done for you.

The reliables –
consistent-quality wines, year in, year out
Several of the most consistent performers in previous editions of *Quaff* have failed to perform this year. Of those that remain, Yalumba, Fox River, Bleasdale and Chestnut Grove have shown most consistency in recent years.

Buying and Drinking Shiraz Cabernet Blends – Some Tips

Cellaring potential

The performance of the 2002 Fiddlers Creek Shiraz Cabernet in this year's tastings brought home to me just how well these blends can improve with age. It was rated Pretty Good last year – largely because it was fairly unapproachable. Twelve months bottle age has softened the wine, so that it retains depth of flavour and is a much better drink. To find similar wines that should improve with age, look for those with firm finishes or substantial tannins. They are more likely to improve rather than the soft, easy-drinking styles. A short period in the coolest, darkest part of your house could well see you rewarded with wines that are more ready to drink. If you haven't done this before, be sure to monitor any wines you put down by drinking one from time to time.

A classic Aussie blend

Shiraz cabernet blends are a unique Australian red wine style and include some of our great wines: Penfolds Bin 389, Yalumba 'Signature', Majella 'Mallaea' and McWilliams '1877'. All but four Penfolds Granges have a small amount of cabernet to go with their shiraz – although it might be stretching the point to call it a shiraz cabernet blend. The blend is considered unfashionable because it blends a grape from the French region of Bordeaux (cabernet) with one from the Rhône Valley (shiraz). The French can't blend these varieties legally in most parts of the country – although rumour suggests that it was common practice in Bordeaux in earlier times. Anyway, the blend works well in Australia, especially with quaffing wines such as those reviewed here.

◗ BLOODY GOOD

2003 Chestnut Grove 'Tall Timber' Shiraz Cabernet $15.40

For the third year in a row a Chestnut Grove shiraz cabernet has featured in this chapter, proving the Manjimup producer's consistency. The nose had me intrigued more than with any other wine I tasted for *Quaff*. For me, the aroma was very clearly of Indian tea (Darjeeling?). Anyway, it's a succulent red with sweet dark berry fruit, smooth texture and substantial, though fine, ripe tannins.

2002 Fiddlers Creek Shiraz Cabernet $12

What a difference a year makes! Last year the opening comment on this wine was that it was bold and firm. Well, it's still bold and does have substantial tannins but I felt that the wine was drinking much better now than it was 12 months ago. All the benefits of cellaring without any cost to you. As it looks now, I think it's the best wine I've seen under the Fiddlers Creek label: briary, vibrant, deep, rich and concentrated with black cherry, red berry and mint flavours.

2003 Fox River Cabernet Shiraz $14.95

Goundrey's second label has been a consistent performer in *Quaff*, especially with its red wines from the Great Southern. This is soft, juicy and smooth with bright, ripe red berry flavours and a fresh, gentle finish that lingers.

► GOOD

2003 Fox Creek 'Shadows Run' Shiraz CS $12

I'm sure there'll be some who are confused by the similarity between this McLaren Vale winery and Fox River, the second label of Mt Barker's Goundrey. This 'Shadows Run' blend has some of the lush richness we expect of McLaren Vale reds without the depth of flavour that the best of the region can achieve. There's some attractive cedary oak although the very firm tannins suggest that the fruit doesn't quite stand up to its oak treatment. It needs a rich, robust dish such as an oxtail stew to tame those tannins.

2004 Lindemans 'Cawarra' Shiraz Cabernet $6.95

The Cawarra label has done particularly well in this year's *Quaff* tastings, especially with this gem. The 2004 Cawarra Shiraz Cabernet is a delightful red blend that is clean, fresh and vibrant with redcurrant and dark plum flavours, good weight, and more power and concentration than you'd expect at this price. Approachable, even gluggable.

► PRETTY GOOD

2003 Andrew Garrett 'Garrett' Shiraz Cabernet $14

Ripe, red berry flavours, chewy texture – fine with some potato gnocchi and a tomato-based meat sauce.

2002 Bleasdale Shiraz Cabernet $14

A soft, round, easy-drinking Langhorne Creek red that has ripe redcurrant and plum flavours.

2003 Fishbone Cabernet Shiraz $13.95

The best of the second label of Blackwood Wines from the Blackwood Valley in Western Australia's timber country: a pleasant, easy-drinking red with ripe plummy sweet fruit and a savoury finish.

2004 Lindemans 'Bin 55' Shiraz Cabernet $8.95
> Clean, fresh and smooth with redcurrant flavours and a gentle finish.

2004 McWilliams 'Inheritance' Shiraz Cabernet $7
> A pleasant, well-made barbecue red with light, plummy fruit and chewy texture.

2003 Poets Corner Shiraz Cabernet $9.95
> The poet is locally born Henry Lawson and this blend comes from Orlando Wyndham's outpost at Mudgee. This is the best vintage for years and is packed with dense, ripe dark fruit, sweet oak and grippy tannins. Quaff away with a rich winter stew.

2002 Taylors 'Promised Land' Shiraz Cabernet $13.95
> This is for lovers of oaky young reds only: supple, smooth and robust with ripe plummy fruit and firm vanillin oak to finish.

2003 Yalumba 'Oxford Landing' Cabernet Shiraz $7.95
> A clean, lively quaffer with reasonably concentrated, ripe red berry flavours and a pleasing grip to finish.

OTHER RED BLENDS

Looks like it's a roller coaster ride for followers of this chapter in *Quaff*. Last year, it was less than half the size of 2003 in spite of a record number of entries. This year the number of wines submitted is down but the quality is sky-high, so the number of wines reviewed is way up. It's not hard to make the link with the current glut of red wine – which means bargains galore for canny wine lovers (that is, those who buy *Quaff*).

When I was tasting a bracket for this chapter, I hit a purple patch: four reds all with deep dark berry flavours, smooth texture and soft, fine, ripe, restrained tannins. They all showed impeccable balance between their fruit and gentle oak treatment. At the time, I thought that surely that's one reason why these red blends can be great quaffers. When the oak is held back, the fruit can shine.

Naturally, those four reds are rated Bloody Good. Not surprisingly, all of the wines with that rating are made by companies keen to establish a presence in this segment of the market. There appears to be some care taken in the making of the wines rather than just treating them as bin-ends for whatever red grapes are left over.

Generally, consumers are preferring straight varietals (especially shiraz and merlot) and these are currently easier to sell than blends. A look at this chapter suggests that because red blends are unfashionable, they can be bargains.

The reliables –
consistent-quality wines, year in, year out

Peter Lehmann 'Clancys' has been in five out of the six editions of *Quaff* and is the only wine featured in this chapter with such an extensive record for consistency.

Buying and Drinking Other Red Blends – Some Tips

Labelling blends

By Australian law, wine may be labelled a straight varietal if it contains 85 per cent or more of that grape variety. If a blend has more than 15 per cent of another variety (or varieties), it (or they) must be named. For example, a wine that is 60 per cent cabernet sauvignon, 30 per cent merlot, 10 per cent petit verdot may be labelled cabernet merlot – or cabernet merlot petit verdot.

The order in which the grape varieties appear on a label indicates which variety makes the largest contribution to the blend. So a shiraz merlot cabernet will be mostly shiraz, with the smallest part of the blend being cabernet.

Cabernet in this chapter is cabernet sauvignon rather than cabernet franc or ruby cabernet.

Drink now

These are reds made for early consumption. You'll notice that most of those reviewed are from the 2004 and 2003 vintages. They'll still be drinking well in a year or two but won't be improved by cellaring. Many have a slight tannic grip on the finish. Consume these with a slow-cooked lamb roast, a hearty beef casserole or some spicy sausages and they'll slip down with the greatest of ease.

▆▶ BLOODY GOOD

2004 Nepenthe 'Tryst' Cabernet Tempranillo Zinfandel $14

It's an unusual blend of varieties: as well as cabernet sauvignon, which gives the wine minty blackcurrant fruit, perfume and fine, grippy tannins, there's also a splodge of tempranillo for its round cherry fruit, and zinfandel for lift and spice. Despite their remarkably diverse ethnic backgrounds (France, Spain, and California/southern Italy, respectively) the three varieties get along in model multicultural fashion inside this bottle, producing a dangerously easy-to-drink, yet sophisticated and elegant – and very well-priced – Friday evening red. Why aren't more winemakers in Australia being this adventurous with their blends and their thinking?

2003 Pikes 'Luccio' Sangiovese Cabernet Petit Verdot $15

This is the most charming of the quaffing reds blends that the Clare Valley's Pikes have made featuring sangiovese. The blend is scarcely conventional but it works wonderfully well. There is round, smooth approachability, squishy, juicy, dark berry flavours and some briary savoury character – no doubt from the sangiovese. Perfect with wood-fired oven pizza.

2004 Pillar Box Red Cabernet Shiraz Merlot $12

The Longbottoms are long-time grape growers and farmers in Padthaway who have recently begun making wine under the Henry's Drive label – primarily for the US market – with great success. This new label should be a big hit given the concentration of flavour and weight of this blend of cabernet, shiraz and merlot – and the price.

2004 Zonte's Footstep Cabernet Malbec $14.95
THE 2006 OBERON KANT MEMORIAL AWARD FOR
THE ULTIMATE AUSTRALIAN WINE UNDER $10 and

THE QUAFF 2006 'Fillet Steak and Chips'
RED WINE OF THE YEAR AWARD
How good is this! Zonte's Footstep is a relatively new label,
which uses fruit from a 210-hectare vineyard in Langhorne
Creek and involves marketer Zar Brooks, viticulturist Geoff
Hardy, winemaker Ben Riggs, and vigneron John Pargeter.
The 2003 vintage of Zonte's Footstep Cabernet Malbec was
pleasant enough but lacked the vibrance and depth of
flavour of this. Here is quintessential quaffing: rich,
densely concentrated cassis, raspberry and red plum
flavours, fleshy texture, ripe, fine tannins nicely balanced
with refreshing acidity. Delicious.

 GOOD

2002 Dal Broi 'Red Hill' Cabernet Shiraz Merlot $8.95
An approachable Riverina red that is fresh and lively, even
vibrant, with a slightly tannic grip.

2004 Fishers Circle Shiraz Merlot Cabernet Sauvignon $12.95
This is a new Southcorp label from Margaret River. No
doubt the fruit is sourced by the team at Devil's Lair and
the wine is made there – but the style and price point is
different from the Devil's Lair 'Fifth Leg'. I like the balance
of the wine: there's plenty of fruit, not too much oak. So it's
a good drink: sweet dark berry fruit, smooth and gluggable.

2003 Houghton Cabernet Shiraz Merlot $10.50
A gold medal at the Griffith Show is a good sign at this
price. The wine has some concentration and depth of dark
berry flavour, smooth texture and substantial, though fine,
ripe tannins.

2004 Zilzie Cabernet Merlot Petit Verdot $15

This is made in a style that polarises opinion. The oak treatment dominates the wine from its fragrant vanilla bean aromas (quite beguiling, in fact) to the noticeable vanillin oak on the finish. It's soft and fleshy, so if you like your reds robust and oaky, this is for you.

▄▶ PRETTY GOOD

2002 Coriole 'Contour 4' Sangiovese Shiraz $14.50
2003 Coriole 'Contour 4' Sangiovese Shiraz $14.50

A bin-end label for this McLaren Vale boutique, which has been a pioneer of sangiovese for more than 20 years. There's a hint of sangiovese's savoury character in this supple, gently flavoured red with a clean and lively finish. I marginally preferred the 2003.

2002 De Bortoli 'Windy Peak' Cabernet Shiraz Merlot $12.95

A pleasant, well-made red with ripe flavours and smooth texture.

2004 Gapsted 'Victorian Alps' Dolcetto Syrah $14.95

Alluring wild berry flavours before a very sweet finish. If you enjoy sweetness, you'll love it.

2003 Peter Lehmann 'Clancy's' Shiraz Cabernet Merlot $14.95

Powerfully flavoured with smooth texture – a reliable Barossa blend.

2004 Rutherglen Estates 'The Reunion'
Mourvedre Shiraz Grenache $14.95

A pleasant, straightforward red with smooth red berry flavours.

2004 Rutherglen Estates 'Red' Shiraz Durif $12.95

An easy-drinking quaffer made from shiraz and durif.

2003 Scarpantoni 'School Block' Shiraz Cabernet Merlot $14.95

This is McLaren Vale: robust and substantial with heaps of
tannins – but approachable for all that with plenty of ripe
fruit.

2003 Tall Poppy Merlot Cabernet Shiraz $13.95

An easy-drinking red from Mildura.

Kisses sweeter than wine

Sweet wines under $15

SWEET WINES UNDER $15

There are two sections to this chapter: 'sweet wines' – the fresher, lighter styles made from late-harvest aromatic grapes, such as muscat, verdelho and riesling; and 'very sweet' wines – the lush dessert wines (or 'stickies'), which are made from much riper, more sugary, shrivelled grapes. Generally, the grapes for these have been infected with 'noble rot' (*Botrytis cinerea*), which speeds up the shrivelling and concentrates the grape sugars. This has the effect of significantly sweetening and concentrating the wines and contributes a rich apricot and marmalade flavour to them. This year we've seen significantly less of this style than in other years. The selection of sweet wines is stronger than usual in spite of a wonderful group of moscatos being moved to their rightful place in the Sweet Sparkling chapter.

The reliables –
consistent-quality wines, year in, year out

Let's hear the fanfare for Brown Brothers, **the** reliable producer of Australian sweet wines under $15. Their classic sweetie, Brown Brothers Spatlese Lexia, has appeared in all six editions of *Quaff*, while the Moscato (reviewed in the chapter on Sweet Sparkling) has made five of six editions. The 2004 Orange Muscat and Flora is reviewed in the short section on Very Sweet Wines.

Buying and Drinking Sweet Wines – Some Tips

Drink young

By far the best time to taste these sweet wines is in the lively vibrance of youth when the wine's primary flavours are at their fruitiest. Drink slightly chilled and enjoy.

Matching sweet wines with food

How do you decide what dessert you will serve with these sweet wines? It depends entirely on how light or heavy the wine is. The simple rule is that the lighter and less sweet the wine is, the lighter and less sweet the dessert should be. Conversely, the heavier and sweeter the wine, the sweeter the dessert should be.

So with the sweet wines you might try fruit salad, pavlova or fruit-based soufflés, and with the very sweet wines heavier desserts such as creme brulee, bread and butter pudding, or sticky date pudding will do very nicely indeed.

All you need are half bottles

One of the ways in which you can tell the difference between sweet and very sweet wines is that the latter are invariably sold in half bottles. On most occasions, a half bottle of dessert wine will be enough for a dinner party. It is sweeter and richer than a full bottle of table wine or even sweet wine. And at the time of the meal we usually serve stickies, our appetites are beginning to flag.

Sweet Wines

➤ GOOD

2005 Angove's 'Butterfly Ridge' Spatlese Lexia $5.95

A fresh, lively, light-bodied sweet white from the Riverland that has sweet grapey flavours and clean, refreshing acidity to finish.

2005 Paul Conti 'Fronti' Muscat $14.95

This fragrant sweetie makes regular appearances in *Quaff* thanks to its alluring grapey perfumes, fresh, clean muscaty flavours and crisp, zingy finish. Perfect as a summer's day quaffer or at any time with a fresh fruit salad.

2005 Rosemount Estate Traminer Riesling $10.95

Wonderfully aromatic, sweet grapey flavours, clean fresh and sweet to finish.

➤ PRETTY GOOD

2004 Brown Brothers Spatlese Lexia $12

While quite restrained on the nose, this is grapey, viscous and very sweet.

2004 Buckland Gap Traminer Riesling $9

Straightforward sweetie that is bright and fresh.

2005 Jim Barry 'Lavender Hill' Riesling $12

A regular in *Quaff*: floral, gentle lemony notes, good depth of flavour and soft, sweet, lingering finish.

2002 Lillypilly Lexia $13.95

From a small (by local standards) winery at Griffith comes this soft, round sweetie with some attractive fragrance and pleasing tropical fruit flavours.

NV McWilliams 'Inheritance' Fruitwood $7

> Attractive sweet flavours with cleansing acidity, feels good in the mouth.

2003 Pertaringa Final Fronti $14.95

> Warm areas such as McLaren Vale do well with these heady aromatic whites. Muscaty, grapey, thick, viscous texture and pleasingly sweet finish. Seductive.

2004 Schild Estate Frontignac $14

> An aromatic Barossa white with heaps of intense grapey flavours – a touch of sweetness on a crisp, lively finish.

Very Sweet Wines

➤ PRETTY GOOD

2004 Brown Brothers Orange Muscat and Flora (375 ml) $9.90

This is a blend unique to Brown Brothers of the rare aromatic French variety, orange muscat, and an American cross between gewürztraminer and semillon. It is subtly muscaty with attractive sweet fruit, smooth and easy-drinking with a clean, sweet finish.

1999 Tollana Botrytis Riesling (375 ml) $14

A dense, lush sticky with intense limey flavours – quite developed at this stage and probably past its best.

Good enough for the vicar

Fortified wines under $15

FORTIFIED WINES
UNDER $15

Until last year, it had seemed that fortifieds represented the most unfashionable segment of the wine market and so this chapter typically abounded in lots of wonderful bargains. Both last year and this, it has appeared that there isn't the same breadth and depth available on the Australian market for less than $15. Choose carefully, and there are still wines that are excellent bargains and very good wines. However, it's harder than it was.

There are now a significant number of outstanding fortifieds available for just over $15, as can be seen by the substantial increase in those reviewed in our Over $15 section. Other wines that we came across in our *Quaff* tastings that just miss out on our $15 price point include the Beelgara VOTP and the Bailey's 'Founder' Muscat and Tokay – each of which is worth seeking out.

The reliables –
consistent-quality wines, year in, year out

The only two fortified wines to have appeared in every edition of *Quaff* are the two Penfolds gems: the Club Tawny and the Reserve Club Aged Tawny. Between them – and under slightly different names (Penfolds Club Port and Penfolds Reserve Bin 421) – they won all our fortified awards until last year. The Reserve Club Aged Tawny has never been rated below Bloody Good, an outstanding achievement.

Buying and Drinking Fortified Wines – Some Tips

Unfashionable, therefore cheap

Tougher drink-driving laws and great consciousness of drinking in moderation are partly responsible for fortified wines becoming unfashionable. This has meant that many of the wines in this chapter are available at bargain basement prices. It has also meant that some wine lovers are paying more for fortifieds but drinking less of them. This may help explain why many of the terrific fortifieds are reviewed in the Over $15 section of *Quaff.*

Plan your dinner party to include fortifieds

One of the reasons for fortifieds losing their appeal is that appetites often wane before we reach the stage of the meal where they come into their own. Plan to drink a freshly opened, slightly chilled dry sherry as an aperitif – with either freshly shucked oysters or lightly grilled prawns. Serve an opulent muscat with a paneforte-style cake (such as New Norcia Nut Cake) for dessert or a flourless chocolate cake with an intense tawny and a short black.

Port

 **BLOODY GOOD**

Brown Brothers Reserve Port $14.10

It looked a bargain last year and has come up trumps in the tastings again this year. Intense butterscotch, honeycomb and treacle, silky texture, good weight and a fine finish that lingers.

Penfolds Club Reserve Aged Tawny $12.95

Omnipresent and the best fortified pretty much all of that time – except for one year in which an excess of spirit enabled its sibling to take top spot. It's been said in each edition of *Quaff*, this is remarkable value for money. You taste the wines blind and this comes up trumps one more time. Penfolds have been making this reserve wine since 1985 from shiraz, grenache and mourvedre. Powerfully flavoured, complex, multi-dimensional, this is opulent and yet fine, with butterscotch, treacle and malt flavours and a neatly balanced finish.

Rossetto Brothers Tawny Port $9

A label of Beelgara, which reflects the origins of the Griffith winery, and better value than the Beelgara VOTP, though that's an impressive fortified in its own right. This has rich, concentrated molasses, treacle and butterscotch flavours, velvety texture and a fine gentle finish with butterscotch and malt lingering. A bargain.

 GOOD

Hardys 'Whiskers Blake' Port $14.95

A restrained fortified with tight structure, silky texture and heaps of flavour.

McWilliams 'Hanwood' Classic Tawny $10.95

> Round and easy to drink with some treacle and honey flavours that linger.

Penfolds Club Tawny $8.95

> One of the Reliables scores well in the tasting once again: soft, round and balanced with treacle and butterscotch flavours. Smooth and satisfying. Outstanding value.

Wolf Blass 'Red Label' Tawny Port $11

> An attractive tawny with treacle, malt and honey characters, lush texture and fine, gentle spirit to finish.

▶ PRETTY GOOD

Angoves 'Anchorage' Old Tawny $11.40

> Some toffee characters, an almost lush texture and quite strong spirit.

Buller 'Victoria' Tawny $10

> This needed a few swirls to clean it up but after that it showed plum and raisin flavours and a soft, round finish.

Sherry

 GOOD

All Saints Golden Cream Sherry $15.50

Sweet, honeyed and syrupy, with malt and butterscotch flavours and a sweet finish in which the alcohol is controlled.

McWilliams 'Hanwood' Amontillado Sherry $10.95

Attractive rancio characters on the nose, treacle-like flavours and very dry finish showing fine yet powerful spirit.

Mildara Chestnut Teal Oloroso $8

This was looking good last year and so it's no surprise that it's come up well again in the tastings. It is rich and concentrated with almost lush texture and an ultra-dry finish that shows delicate balance with the alcohol.

 PRETTY GOOD

McWilliams 'Hanwood' Oloroso Sherry $10.95

Intense and fine with rancio characters and dry, balanced finish.

Mildara Rio Vista Dry Sherry $8

Rancio characters on nose, soft, round and gentle with dry finish.

Mildara Supreme Dry Sherry $8

Not as intense as some but soft, round, easy-drinking style.

Muscat and Tokay

➤ BLOODY GOOD

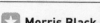 **Morris Black Label Liqueur Muscat** $11.95

> THE QUAFF 2006 'Any Port in a Storm'
> FORTIFIED WINE OF THE YEAR AWARD
> A sensational Rutherglen muscat for less than $15! A terrific fortified by the master blender David Morris, which has typical grapey, raisiny character, is suprisingly rich and concentrated (for the price), has that irrestible lush, velvety texture and a gentle raisiny finish that lingers.

➤ GOOD

Buller 'Victoria' Muscat $10

> I'm always banging on about what great value Australian fortifieds are – with good reason. Because they are unfashionable, Aussie fortifieds often represent outstanding value. Andrew Buller is a fourth-generation winemaker from Rutherglen who makes some terrific regional fortifieds – the best of which are priced according to their rarity. This muscat is released under Buller's quaffing label – Victoria – and is a good wine at a very reasonable price. It is soft, round and light-bodied, has a pleasant sweetness, some raisiny character and makes delicious easy drinking.

McWilliams 'Hanwood' Classic Muscat $10.95

> As impressive as it was last year: light-bodied, fresh and round; soft, round and fruity; with ripe grapey, raisiny flavours and spirit on the finish that is a little too strong.

➤ PRETTY GOOD

Buller 'Victoria' Tokay $10

> Velvety with toffee and malt flavours and a soft, round, easy finish.

Angoves 'Bookmark' Marsala $4.95
> Strong vanilla perfumes, very sweet, very strong vanilla flavours to finish.

Stones Green Ginger Wine $8.95
> This has lively ginger beer aromas, is soft and sweet and manages to avoid being cloying.

An affair to remember

Imported wines under $20

IMPORTED WINES UNDER $20

There continues to be a boom in the sales of imported wines into Australia. Sommeliers are delighting in the opportunity to teach their customers about exciting new flavours and wine styles from overseas. The independent retailers are seeing overseas wines as an area in which they can compete with the large chains – especially by targeting some of the smaller producers. And, as you'll see from this chapter, the big guys such as Vintage Cellars are actively bringing in some bargain buys, especially from France and Italy. There is a great deal available between $15 and $20 from overseas wineries and only a limited amount under $15, so you'll understand why the $20 price point works better for these wines.

For contact details of each importer, refer to the section 'Finding the Wines' on page 202.

The reliables –
consistent-quality wines, year in, year out

The sparkling wines of Grandin, Riccadonna and Mondoro have been regulars in *Quaff*, as have the table wines of Vidal Fleury (France) and Umani Ronchi (Italy).

Buying and Drinking Imported Wines – Some Tips

Travel the world

There can't be many readers of this book who don't regularly eat in restaurants or cafes that feature a range of different cuisines – Italian, Greek, French, Chinese, Thai, Vietnamese ... And I'll bet that the majority of us cook dishes from lots of different countries. We all love something different, a new taste experience, something to tantalise. Trying imported wines is a bit like that, broadening one's horizons, learning a bit more about the infinite possibilities that wine offers. One of the things that I love when I'm overseas is trying the local wines. Being able to enjoy them when I'm back in Australia helps rekindle those memories – as well as providing an opportunity for me to try something different.

Great food wines

Most of the wines from countries such as France, Italy and Spain are just made to go with food. In these places, grapes have been grown for hundreds of years and a local cuisine has grown up alongside the region's wines. They can sometimes look pretty ordinary when tasted by themselves, but are transformed with food. You might also like to try appropriate food and wine from the same country: a French provencial stew with a hearty red from the Côtes du Ventoux; your perfect spaghetti bolognese with a rustic Chianti; a Spanish white with a robust paella.

Imported Sparkling

▶ BLOODY GOOD

Grandin Brut, France $14.95

Much better than it was last year, the Grandin is intense, has good weight and feels good in the mouth. It has a tight, steely structure and a powerful, zippy, dry finish of considerable length. Imported by Tucker Seabrook (now called Fine Wine Partners).

Riccadonna Asti Spumante, Italy $15.95

It may be commercially successful and popular because it's a sweetie but don't let that put you off – this came up trumps in the tastings. The grapey, muscaty aromas are voluminous, just wonderful; it has some plumpness in the mid-palate but is tight and fine with crisp drying acidity that balances the sweetness wondrously well. It feels great in the mouth, is initially sweet and, rather than being cloying, is actually fresh and lively. Imported by Southcorp.

▶ GOOD

Cora Asti Spumante, Italy $10.79

Attractive grapey flavours, pleasantly sweet with a crisp, clean, sweet finish. Imported by Vintage Cellars.

Deutz Marlborough Brut Cuvee, New Zealand $21.95

Over the price point and will appeal to some, though not all. It's a question of style: you love it or not. Robust, developed, yeasty, big, bold with heaps of character. Imported by Montana.

Lindauer Special Reserve, New Zealand $17.95

There's just a slight touch of blush making it (at least) rosé-like: it has yeasty, bready characters, a good mouthfeel and crisp, zesty acidity. Good fizz. Imported by Montana.

Mondoro Asti Spumante, Italy $14.95

Musk stick and grapey fragrances with some honeysuckle, it is soft, round and sweet. Could do with a touch more acidity to balance, but if you like sweet, here it is. Imported by McWilliams.

▰ PRETTY GOOD

Grandin Rosé, France $14.95

This has some musk stick aromas, is clean, fresh and sweet with strawberry flavours and a lively finish. Imported by Fine Wine Partners.

Lindauer Fraise, New Zealand $15.95

This has natural strawberries added so you might not be surprised by the fairy-floss fragrances and musk flavours: it is soft, round and very sweet – much too sweet. I might have known it would be a best seller! Only if you have a very sweet tooth. Imported by Montana.

Tosti Moscato d'Asti, Italy $17.50

There's only a gentle sparkle here to complement wonderful fragrances, attractive sweet grapey flavours and a gentle, soft finish with crisp acidity. Just a touch too sweet for me, but many will love it. Imported by Arquilla.

Imported Whites

BLOODY GOOD

2003 Masi 'Levarie' Soave, Italy $19.95

This blend of garganega (85 per cent) and trebbiano (15 per cent) is largely unoaked, although a small portion is given time in old oak casks. Careful viticulture and August rains in the Veneto reduced the impact of the warm conditions pre-vintage. Beautifully fragrant, soft and juicy with a pleasant balanced mouthfeel, a hint of cedary oak and cashew nuts, and delicate, refreshing acidity. Imported by Red & White.

2003 Montana 'Reserve' Chardonnay, New Zealand $19.95

A terrific Kiwi chardonnay at this price: intense cedary oak aromas and rich, concentrated melon, white peach and nectarine flavours. Oak dominates the finish. Imported by Montana.

2004 Montana Sauvignon Blanc, New Zealand $15.95
2005 Montana Sauvignon Blanc, New Zealand $15.95

In most years, it's impossible to go past this as the best value-for-money sauvignon to come out of New Zealand. While many of the sauvignons that I've seen from the 2004 vintage (Cloudy Bay and Framingham have been noticeable exceptions) have lacked their usual punch, this Montana is up with the best of the brand – and, at the price, represents wonderful value. It has the fresh pungency, pristine fruit purity and vibrant, taut, zippy acidity (that you expect from Kiwi sauvignon) together with sweet lychee and gooseberry flavours balanced by refreshing, cool minerality. Imported by Montana.

2003 Torres 'Vina Esmeralda', Spain $15.95
THE QUAFF 2006 'An Affair to Remember'
IMPORTED WHITE WINE OF THE YEAR AWARD
This is sourced from the mountainous area of the Upper
Penedes using the heady aromatic varieties moscatel and
gewürztraminer – as becomes immediately obvious when
you open the bottle. This is wonderfully fragrant, has pristine grapey, muscaty flavours, and a gentle fruity finish that
lingers. Serve chilled. Imported by the Spanish acquisition.

▶ GOOD

2004 Mount Riley Sauvignon Blanc, New Zealand $15.95
A well-made, medium-bodied sauvignon with light, rather
than intense, tropical flavours (gooseberries and lychees),
which build up in the glass before crisp, cleansing acidity.
Very good value. Imported by Angoves.

2003 Ruffino 'Lumina del Borgo' Pinot Grigio, Italy $13.49
I loved the over-the-top ripe, almost overripe, flavours,
which reminded me of that most pungent of Asian tropical
fruits, durian. Interesting, intriguing. Imported by Vintage
Cellars.

2004 Selaks Sauvignon Blanc, New Zealand $15.30
There's heaps of fruit in this aromatic, even pungent,
sauvignon with grassy, herbal flavours, viscous texture and
a finish that shows a touch of sweetness. Imported by
Vintage Cellars.

► PRETTY GOOD

2004 Domaine du Tariquet Cotes de Gascogne Ugni Blanc Colombard, France $14.95

An interesting white from the south-west of France that shows gentle apple and lemon flavours. Try it with duck or pork rillettes and some thinly sliced, toasted sourdough bread. Imported by the Prince Wine Store.

2004 Normanno Inzolia, Italy $16.80

This is a straightforward unoaked white made from the indigenous grape variety, inzolia, sourced from Trapani on the west coast of Sicily. It is soft, round and very easy-drinking with a dry, savoury finish. Like most of these, it is at its best with food – such as deep-fried salt-and-pepper squid. Imported by Enoteca Sileno.

2005 Stoneleigh Sauvignon Blanc, New Zealand $17.95

After being quite subdued to start, the flavours build in the glass so it becomes fruitier with more overt tropical flavours. Imported by Montana.

2003 Umani Ronchi 'Villa Bianchi' Verdicchio, Italy $15.95

Umani Ronchi is based in the Marches region on the eastern coast of central Italy. This 100 per cent verdicchio is sourced from the Verdicchio Classico area and is an excellent entry-level white: delicately floral with restrained apple and pear characters, good weight, and a clean, dry finish that lingers. Imported by Trembath & Taylor.

2004 White Island Semillon Sauvignon Blanc, New Zealand $17.95

A pleasant, easy-drinking white blend with some spicy, melony flavours and gentle, fresh acidity. Imported by Montana.

Imported Reds

📢 **BLOODY GOOD**

2003 Cantine Rallo 'Spirita di Rallo' Nero d'Avola Cabernet, Italy $19.80

Cantine Rallo was established in 1860 in Sicily and currently has 60 hectares under vine in the Alcamo region best known for its white wines. This red has been sourced more widely from the province of Trapani at the western end of Sicily. It is an unwooded blend of the local variety nero d'avola (70 per cent) and cabernet sauvignon (30 per cent). Characteristically, nero d'avola is soft and robust – an easy-drinking style. This is right in the mould: generous, fleshy, mulberry and dark plum flavours with some robust earthy notes and a long, dry finish. Imported by Enoteca Sileno.

2002 Domaines Perrin La Vieille Ferme 'Lasira', France $14

This label is owned by the Perrin family, which has Chateauneuf du Pape's outstanding Chateau Beaucastel. The wine is sourced from the Languedoc Roussillon's eastern-most region – Costieres-de-Nîmes – which is north of the town of Nîmes and the Camargue. It is a medium-bodied blend of syrah (shiraz) and grenache (80:20), has intense red cherry and red plum flavours, soft, smooth texture, plenty of approachable tannins, and a dry, savoury finish. An attractive French red at a good price. Sealed with a screwcap – and so, as the back label says, contains 0 per cent cork. Imported by Negociants.

⭐ **2004 La Belle Terrasse Shiraz, France** $13.95

THE QUAFF 2006 'Another Foreign Affair'
IMPORTED RED WINE OF THE YEAR AWARD

An impeccably clean, vibrant shiraz – from the Languedoc Roussillon in the south of France – that has juicy, even squishy, raspberry and plum flavours, before a nicely balanced finish. Imported by Southcorp.

2004 Oyster Bay Merlot, New Zealand $18.95

>This is a surprise packet from Hawke's Bay – aromatic, ripe and plummy with impressive richness and concentration, silky texture and a pleasing grip to finish. Value. Imported by Oyster Bay.

▶ GOOD

2004 Castello di Gabbiano Chianti, Italy $15.95

>A good entry-level chianti: soft, round, smooth with lively savoury flavours (beetroot, satsuma plums). Cries out for a dish such as spaghetti with a robust Bolognese ragu. Imported by Beringer Blass.

2003 Cerro del Masso Chianti, Italy $19.95

>Here is a very good chianti from the warm 2003 vintage: ripe, red-skin fruits, smoothly textured, with savoury, even earthy, characters, neat balance and substantial, fine, chalky tannins. Great with a hearty saltimboca. Imported by the Prince Wine Store.

2003 Domaines Perrin La Vieille Ferme Cotes du Ventoux Rose, France $16

>Comes from the south of France – close to the setting of Peter Mayle's *A Year in Provence*. Delicate, earthy, wild strawberry flavours: fresh and dry to finish. Imported by Negociants.

2003 M Chapoutier 'Bila Haut' Cotes de Roussillon, France $16

>Also from the Languedoc Roussillon, this is a light- to medium-bodied red that has red berry flavours and is tight, lean and dry. As with all these reds, much improved by drinking with a meal. Imported by Chapoutier.

2004 Stoneleigh Marlborough Pinot Noir, New Zealand $17.95

There were spicy, black pepper aromas, which I associate more with shiraz than pinot noir, but beguiling anyway. The texture is very much pinot: smooth, supple with persistent flavours and a soft, gentle finish. Very attractive at the price. Imported by Montana.

2004 Twin Islands Pinot Noir, New Zealand $19.95

Well-priced for a Marlborough pinot – perfumed, ripe raspberry, red cherry, tamarillo flavours, vibrant and almost silky smooth. Imported by Yalumba.

▬► PRETTY GOOD

2003 Montana 'Reserve' Pinot Noir, New Zealand $19.95

A good quaffing pinot with savoury (sour cherry, beetroot) flavours and smooth texture. Imported by Montana.

2004 Mount Riley Pinot Noir, New Zealand $18.95

A pleasant, smooth pinot without the depth of some of the others reviewed here. Imported by Angoves.

2004 Solo Arte Sangiovese, Italy $9.50

There is some robust winemaking along with good red berry flavours in this Italian cheapie. Imported by Arquilla.

2003 Vidal Fleury Cotes du Ventoux, France $13.45

A pleasant French country red that has earthy, savoury flavours and very smooth texture. Imported by Vintage Cellars.

Lash out

Great-value wines over $15

GREAT-VALUE WINES OVER $15

Most people most of the time, either through necessity or choice, don't want to spend more than $15 on a bottle of wine. And that is clearly the focus of this book. However, there will be times when you can't resist the temptation to spend a bit more – it may be something you do for dinner on weekends or for special occasions, or you might share more expensive bottles with wine-loving friends to expand your knowledge of wines.

So this section of the book contains a list of all kinds of wines that are over our $15 limit. In many cases, I saw them as part of the *Quaff* tastings – and found subsequently that they had a recommended retail price about $15. However, there are many outstanding bargains that I saw as part of my normal work as a wine writer – in particular as part of my regular new release tastings. As always with *Quaff*, I am recommending the crème de la crème, the wines that stood out – firstly for reasons of quality, and only secondly because they represent good value.

Buying Wines Over $15 – Some Tips

Be alert

With changes on the Australian retail scene, especially connected with the expansion of Coles and Woolworths (under all their different shopfronts), nothing stays the same. Discounting and special deals are very much part of daily life. Keep an eye on newspaper advertising to see if any of the wines recommended here are available as specials. You may well find that some of the wines I believe are good value for $18–$20 are available on special below $15, and some that we recommended at $22–$25 are on sale for less than $20. There are no rules, especially with loss leaders.

Your friend, the wine merchant

There are significant advantages in establishing a relationship with a wine merchant, especially a local one, and channelling all or most of your wine purchases through him or her. They'll certainly keep you informed of any special deals (whether on price or the availability of rare or difficult-to-get wines). If there are bargains, you'll hear about them first. If those bargains are in short supply, you can expect to be looked after. Another advantage is that the wine merchant will get to know your taste and that will help him or her in recommending wines to you. Cultivate the friendship.

Sparkling Wines over $15

2001 Hardys 'Sir James' Pinot Noir Chardonnay $23

Another excellent bubbly from arguably the most talented sparkling winemaker in the country, Ed Carr. This has bready, yeasty characters, sumptuous creamy texture and clean, refreshing acidity to finish. Fair price considering the quality.

2002 Heemskerk Pinot Noir Chardonnay $27.95

A grand Tassie bubbly, now a label for direct mailer, Cellarmasters (1800 500 260): delicate lemon citrus characters with a hint of yeast, creamy texture (just marvellous in the mouth) and a fresh, dry finish.

Pol Gessner $36.95

This is significantly cheaper than (I suspect) any other champagne on the Australian market, partly because it is a second label of the largest family-owned Champagne house – Marne et Champagne – and partly because it is directly imported by Woolworths. This non-vintage bubbly won a rare Blue Gold at the 2003 Sydney Top 100 (when I was a judge). Although this would not be the same blend as the Blue Gold winner, that triumph does show the class of this bubbly. It is big, bold and robust with heaps of strong yeasty, toasty, biscuity flavours. Exclusive to BWS.

Woop Woop 'Black Chook' Shiraz $19

It's that Ben Riggs again – and judging by the impossible-to-ignore name – Black Chook – I'm betting that serial namer Zar Brooks was somewhere around too. The wine itself is robust, meaty, and densely flavoured with mid-palate softness, powerful acidity and a lingering aftertaste.

White Wines over $15

2002 Balnaves Chardonnay $28

In the speech announcing Pete Bissell as 2005 Qantas/Gourmet Traveller WINE Winemaker of the Year, Huon Hooke was quoted as saying that the Balnaves Chardonnay as the best in Coonawarra. This is a fine example of how good they can be: it has intense white peach and honeydew melon flavours and a crisp, dry finish of considerable length.

2004 Brown Brothers Pinot Grigio $15.90

A fascinating example of this trendy variety: lavender and dried herb perfumes, savoury, minerally flavours and a lingering dry finish. Mouth-watering.

2005 Capel Vale CV Semillon Sauvignon Blanc $17

This is a stunner from Capel's Rebecca Caitlin and shows the quality of the vast grape-growing resources of Peter and Elizabeth Pratten's winery. Capel Vale own vineyards in Geographe, the Great Southern, Pemberton and Margaret River. The wines show the fresh youthful zestiness and vibrance that the most outstanding examples of this white blend can achieve, especially in Western Australia's coolest regions. There are green bean, green pea, fresh herb flavours, a soft, gentle mouthfeel, good weight and a crisp dry finish that lingers.

2004 Evans & Tate Margaret River Chardonnay $20

A fine, elegant and subtle white with gentle cedary oak, nectarine and stone fruit flavours and refreshing acidity. Well-priced.

2004 Gapsted Ballerina Canopy Sauvignon Blanc $18

Gapsted is starting to make an impact with some outstanding cool climate whites. They are owned by a group of King and Alpine Valley grape-growers and have Michael Cope-Williams as their winemaker This sauvignon is sourced from the King Valley and shows the benefit of the long, cool growing season, picking at night, and extra-long fermentation period (four weeks rather than 10 to 14 days). It has intense pristine white peach, nectarine, lychee and guava flavours, fleshy texture and crisp refreshing acidity. An outstanding sauvignon at a great price.

2004 Juniper Crossing Semillon Sauvignon Blanc $16

A well-priced Margaret River sem sav blanc from a new-ish Wilyabrup producer whose winemaker is Mark Messenger, formerly at Cape Mentelle. This is in the ripe, tropical fruit, passionfruit spectrum, is fresh, clean and vibrant. There are lovely passionfruit characters that linger on the finish.

2004 Knappstein 'Three' $20

This is a fascinating new white blend from the Clare Valley's Knappstein – no doubt inspired by similar blends of gewürztraminer, riesling and pinot gris from France's north-eastern province of Alsace. It's not dissimilar to Hugel's Gentil – *Quaff* 2004's Imported White Wine of the Year. Knappstein's departing general manager, Andrew Hardy, has moved back to take over the reins at Petaluma after a decade in the Clare. He would be at pains to point out that these three varieties have proved themselves in Clare. That is certainly true of riesling and gewürztraminer: and I see no reason why pinot gris shouldn't work perfectly well – we just haven't seen very much so far. This is a robust, powerful white that shows layer after layer of flavour – lime, citrus, Turkish delight – before a crisp, fresh finish softened by a touch of residual sugar.

2004 Leasingham 'Bin 7' Riesling $18

An outstanding riesling from the Clare Valley: clearly focused, delicate yet with layer after layer of intense lemony, limey flavours. Pure, fruity, dry, refreshing.

2004 Madfish Riesling $16

You want to know what fruit purity is? Take a look at the latest Madfish Riesling. Incredible pristine lime juice that is fresh and succulent on the mid-palate and lingers. It is fine and tightly structured and yet is vibrant, fleshy and dry. There is some restraint with complex mineral notes, which ensures that the finish shows sublime finesse and bright refreshing acidity. It won three trophies at the 2004 Qantas Mount Barker Wine Show of Western Australia: Best White Wine, Best Riesling and the Gladstones Trophy for the wine showing the most distinctive regional character. Not bad for a wine that sells for $16 a bottle. It's sourced from the Porongurups and Mount Barker sub-regions of the Great Southern. Here's hoping that Mike Kerrigan and the team from Howard Park's Madfish label can repeat the dose in future years.

2004 Mistletoe Reserve Chardonnay $23

Winner of Wine of the Show at the 2005 Boutique Wine Awards for this Hunter Valley winery. It's an impressive chardonnay that is fragrant with buttery, peachy, cedary oak flavours, an attractive mouthfeel, and good depth and length. Available at the cellar door and directly from the winery.

2004 Montana 'Reserve' Sauvignon Blanc $19.95

I've been impressed by both Montana wines from 2004 – especially this Reserve. There's heaps of bold ripe gooseberry and lychee tropical flavours, a fresh vibrance and lingering zesty acidity.

2004 Mount Majura Chardonnay $20

The nine hectare Mount Majura vineyard is situated in the ACT just 11 km from the national capital on the slopes of the mountain of the same name. One hectare of pinot noir, merlot and chardonnay was established in 1988 and these plantings have been extended since Mount Majura was taken over by a syndicate that includes viticulturist and winemaker Frank van de Loo. Their Chardonnay will not appeal to everyone but if you like a leaner, more austere, cool climate white, this may well be of interest. It is tight with cool, minerally flavours and a firm, even grippy, finish. Different and well-priced.

2004 Mount Majura Pinot Gris $16

At Mount Majura pinot gris and riesling were planted in 2000 on the red volcanic soil of the Pines Block and already show huge promise. Delicately fragrant with pear, spice and apple flavours, this is a fresh, clean, lively expression of the variety which is viscous, has impressive richness, depth and length of flavour. Delightfully dry finish. Great value.

2004 Ninth Island Chardonnay $22.50

Don't expect Tassie wines to be cheap or readily available – but don't be surprised if they are of very good quality. This is from Pipers Brook's second label: it is fragrant, ripe, fruity and very appealing.

2004 Palandri Semillon Sauvignon Blanc $16.95

An impressive white from this large, Margaret River-based producer. It has grassy, herbal flavours, is clean and lively, soft and full on the mid-palate, and has refreshing lemony acidity and some tropical notes on a crisp lingering finish.

2004 Petaluma 'Hanelin Hill' Riesling $23

Once again the fact that this quintessential Clare riesling is made in large volumes keeps its price below rieslings of similar quality. Sourced from Petaluma's Hanelin Hill vineyard and inevitably showing regional lime zest, vibrant juiciness and mouth-puckering refreshing acidity.

2003 Punt Road Chardonnay $22

Kate Goodman has made a more complex chardonnay at her Yarra Valley winery: it has an attractive creamy mouthfeel, concentrated peachy, melony fruit with some nutty, minerally notes. Satisfying.

2004 Richmond Grove Riesling $14
2004 Richmond Grove Watervale Riesling $16

That great riesling winemaker John Vickery can still turn on the magic, as his latest two releases from Richmond Grove show. The Watervale Riesling is extremely fine, has delicate flora aromas, intense lemon and lime citrus flavours before a finish that has refreshing zesty acidity that lingers. Vickery believes that it's an each-way bet – and can be gulped now or enjoyed with some bottle age if carefully cellared. Five to seven years will see it gain complexity and develop mature characters, while the screwcap will keep it clean and fresh. Though the Richmond Grove Riesling ($14), sourced from the Barossa and Eden Valleys, is not quite in the class of its twin, it is cheaper and represents good value.

2004 Rockfield Semillon $15.50

This is the best of the releases from a new winery at Rosa Glen to the south of the township of Margaret River. Andrew Gaman (the younger) makes the wines for the family winery and does some consulting to small local wineries. There is an extensive range of cheaply priced wines, which I don't regard as great value because they are made from very young vines – and it's evident. The exceptions are the Semillon Sauvignon Blanc ($15) and this Semillon, which was a gold medal winner at the 2004 Margaret River Show. The 2004 Rockfield Semillon is a clearly focused white with intense fresh herb and grassy characters. It is lively, clean and full of flavour with refreshing acidity that lingers. Mainly cellar door.

2004 Skillogalee Riesling $19.50

This small producer serves one of the best lunches in the Clare Valley and regularly makes one of Australia's top ten rieslings, even in a tricky vintage such as 2004: pristine, lime juice flavours, clearly focused, multi-layered, well-priced.

2005 Torzi Matthews Riesling $23

The first release of an extraordinary, beautifully focused Eden Valley riesling from Tracy Matthews and Domenic Torzi – floral, talc aromas, freshly squeezed lemon juice, zesty limes. Hard to find but worth it: gc@dynastyfinewines.com.au.

2004 Wolf Blass 'Gold Label' Chardonnay $23

This is one of the new wines in the portfolio that is upgrading the image of the Gold Label. (It was pretty well regarded anyway.) Very well-priced for an Adelaide Hills Chardonnay of this quality: cool, intense white peach and nectarine flavours – a complete package showing finesse and vibrance.

Pink Wines over $15

2004 Bay of Fires 'Tigress' Rosé $25

From the second label of Tasmania's Bay of Fires winery, this is a delicate rosé that is fresh, beautifully clean, showing red cherry, strawberry flavours, wonderful viscosity filled out by a hint of sweetness and a gentle, lingering finish.

2004 Blue Pyrenees 'Summer' Rosé $18

A light, juicy rosé with flavours reminiscent of fresh garden herbs and strawberries and a crisp, lively finish.

2004 Charles Melton 'Rosé of Virginia' $18.90

Arguably Australia's quintessential rosé, made by Charlie Melton, who never gets closer to white wine than this. It's predominantly grenache with a little cabernet sauvignon, shiraz and (surprisingly) pinot meunier. This is lean and savoury with deep ripe strawberry flavour and a powerful, dry finish.

2004 Kilikanoon Rosé $18

A lovely dry style from this very impressive Clare Valley label: some herbal notes, fresh, clean and lively with a lingering, dry aftertaste.

2004 Lillydale Rosé $18

There's some attractive primary fruits – raspberry and strawberry – fleshed out by a touch of sweetness and refreshing, crisp acidity.

2004 Pepperjack Grenache Rosé $23

From lovers of dry rosés, this has some floral aromatics, is lean, tight and savoury with a firm, dry, even grippy finish.

2004 Turkey Flat Rosé $19

> The other outstanding Barossa rosé, made from grenache, cabernet, shiraz and dolcetto. It has a lifted floral nose, is clean, fresh and lively with savoury red berry flavours, a hint of mid-palate sweetness and impeccable balance on the long finish.

2004 Wirra Wirra 'Mrs Wigley' Rosé $16.50

> The colourful life and times of Wirra Wirra's winery cat are celebrated in this McLaren Vale rosé. It's made from a blend of petit verdot, grenache and malbec and has attractive fruity aromatics – musk stick, strawberries, raspberries – and succulent sweet fruit brought into balance by crisp, refreshing acidity.

Red Wines over $15

2003 Alkoomi Shiraz Viognier $22

Alkoomi in the Frankland River region of the Great Southern was established in 1971 and has grown considerably in the past 10 years. This is only the second vintage in which they've produced this delicious red – five per cent viognier, added to give a floral lift. Spicy, silky smooth texture, restrained oak, ripe plum flavours: very easy to drink.

2003 Arakoon 'Lighthouse' Cabernet Sauvignon $20

A big, lush McLaren Vale red from this new-ish producer. Heaps of oak but ripe cassis and plum fruit to match; harmonious and approachable.
Try www.ibisman.com.au/arakoon

2001 Balnaves Cabernet Sauvignon $31

The Balnaves flagship 'The Tally' Cabernet was the most impressive wine that I tasted all year and helped winemaker Pete Bissell become Qantas/Gourmet Traveller WINE Winemaker of the Year. It's priced in the stratosphere but the standard Balnaves is a brilliant red at a fair price. The great vintage shows in its spicy, smoky oak, deep cassis flavours, velvety texture, and substantial ripe tannins: for all its power, a wine of finesse and elegance. Excellent value.

2003 Prunotto Barbera d'Alba $23

Prunotto is now owned by the Antinori family but it remains one of the better Piedmont producers. The barbera from Alba in Piedmont in north-eastern Italy is highly regarded. In the 2003, this Barbera d'Alba had gentle, savoury aromas, vibrant fruit, smooth texture and fine lingering tannins.

2002 Barking Owl Shiraz $16

The second label of Perth Hills-based Millbrook, owned by businessman Peter Fogarty, who also owns Lake's Folly in the Hunter and Deep Woods in Margaret River. This is soft, round and smooth with ripe plummy fruit and a fair bit of oak. If that doesn't worry you, it's good value.

2003 Barrecas Shiraz Malbec $16

Although most of their fruit is sold to Houghton, wine-maker sister Iolanda (26) and viticulturist brother Fil Barreca (29) make some excellent, well-priced reds at their Donnybrook winery. This is soft, smooth and medium-bodied with ripe, sweet redcurrant and red cherry flavours and gentle, easy drinking.
Cellar door or mail order: (08) 9731 1716.

2001 Barwang Cabernet Sauvignon $24

A well-priced cabernet from McWilliams' vineyard in the picturesque Hilltops region of New South Wales: fragrant vanillin oak, ripe plummy flavours and pleasing fleshy texture. Approachable now.

2002 Bowen Estate Shiraz $26.99

An excellent year for shiraz in Coonawarra with concentration coming as yields were slashed in half. Black pepper, spicy oak, rich mulberry flavours, velvety texture and fine, ripe tannins.

2002 Brands Cabernet Sauvignon $23

This year saw the sad death of winemaker Jim Brand (53), but his legacy lives on in wines like this powerful, full-bodied red with heaps of oak and substantial fine-grain tannins, which are neatly balanced by rich blackberry fruit. Excellent value for top-class Coonawarra cabernet.

2003 Broomstick Estate Shiraz $16

This new vineyard has produced an appealing red from its six-year-old vines at Witchcliffe, south of the Margaret River township. It has minty, plummy, charry oak flavours and smooth texture. Fair price.

Limited availability: www.broomstick.com.au
or (08) 9757 7777

2002 Brown Brothers Merlot $17.20

Ripe, redcurrant, plum flavours with lush, fleshy texture. Soft, gentle and sweet to finish. Too sweet for me but it will appeal to many.

2003 Cape Mentelle 'Marmaduke' $17

Chances are you'll see this discounted to below $15. It's the Cape Mentelle bin-end red – used to soak up whatever grapes are left over. It is largely shiraz, grenache and mourvedre. It's soft, round, a touch savoury, and made for easy quaffing. Just enjoy. A regular in *Quaff.*

2002 Chateau Tanunda Barossa Tower Shiraz $18

A grand old Barossa winery has been restored to its former glory by businessman (and Cowra Estate owner) John Geber. Winemaker Ralph Fowler has taken up residence and is producing some great value reds such as this: succulent, dark berry and black olive flavours and smooth texture.

2003 Coldstream Hills Merlot $25.95

This is a very impressive Yarra merlot well worth the asking price: gentle, dark plummy flavours, pure sweet fruit, beautifully balanced so that the finish is dry and long.

2003 Cumulus 'Climbing' Merlot $19

From the Central Ranges region at Orange (and therefore grown below 600 m), this new company is headed up by Philip Shaw, with chief winemaker Phil Dowell (formerly of Coldstream Hills). It's a soft, round, easy-drinking style: ripe and plummy with slight grip to finish.

2003 D'Arenberg 'The Cadenzia' Grenache Shiraz Mourvedre $24.95

Who can keep up with McLaren Vale's livewire Chester Osborn and his D'Arenberg juggernaut with its ever expanding portfolio? This is one of the best of the current crop: fragrant, alluring, lush, ripe raspberry and mulberry flavours. So easy to drink.

2002 D'Arenberg 'The Footbolt' Shiraz $22

A fragrant, rich, concentrated McLaren Vale shiraz that shows heaps of red plum, red cherry flavours as well as the region's vibrance and fleshiness. The 2003 is not quite as good but does have concentration and may develop with time.

2003 Ferngrove 'Majestic' Cabernet Sauvignon $24.95

The best yet from the Frankland River's Ferngrove – a gold medal winner at the Perth Show. Cedar, spice, dark berry fruit, velvety texture and firm tannins to finish. Needs some time to soften but is very impressive.

2004 Flying Fish Cove Shiraz $20

The price has risen with the change of vintage and this is very young: in fact, it's likely to need a good swirl to open it up. A ripe, smooth Margaret River red that is still fairly well priced.

2003 Gemtree 'Uncut' Shiraz $25

A dense, smooth and vibrant McLaren Vale shiraz – the vineyard is mature although the label is newly established. Worth trying especially if you enjoy a ripe, jammy edge to your reds.

2003 Gilberts 'Three Devil's' Shiraz $17

Made by Plantagenet for one of Mount Barker's best vineyards, this is the Gilberts' second string shiraz and it's surprisingly rich, concentrated and powerful. Impressive depth of flavour for a wine of this price.

2003 Glaetzer 'Wallace' Shiraz Cabernet Grenache $20

A supple, fleshy, Barossa red blend from the top-flight, father-and-son team of Colin and Ben Glaetzer: rich, deep, full-bodied, comfortable and satisfying.

2002 Gramps Shiraz $16

It may be difficult to find stocks of this remarkably priced Barossa shiraz. The label, which celebrates the Gramps family's contribution to Orlando, hits a high spot with this 2002 shiraz – made possible by a combination of the outstanding, long, cool 2002 vintage plus Orlando's substantial fruit resources. It's rich, ripe, deeply flavoured with dark plums, brambles and spice, generous fleshy texture and a firm but approachable finish. Will improve in the short term but drinking well now.

2003 Juniper Crossing Cabernet Sauvignon $16

This will be the best value Margaret River red on the market when *Quaff 2006* hits the shelves. The price is a metaphor for the times. This is the second label of Juniper Estate – a new (established 1999) Margaret River winery, which took over the 30-year-old vines on the former Wrights' property (opposite Vasse Felix). Those vines have been rejuvenated but the brand is establishing itself – hence the price of this wine, a goodly percentage of which comes from those 30-year-old vines. The 2002 was Good but this 2003 is Bloody Good: velvety, opulent, complex, concentrated ripe cassis and cedary oak, wonderful length.

2002 Kilikanoon 'Killerman's Run' Shiraz $20

This budget label from a very fine Clare Valley producer is not in the class of their best reds (which sell for twice the price). However, this robust, inky black shiraz has power and flavour.

2002 Kilikanoon 'Killerman's Run' Shiraz Grenache $20

One of two good shiraz blends under the 'Killerman's Run' label from this fine Clare Valley producer. It's the grenache that makes this the riper, more fleshy and more lushly flavoured of the two.

2004 Kooyong 'Massale' Pinot Noir $26

Winemaker Sandro Mosele has helped propel Kooyong into the top rank of Mornington Peninsula chardonnay and pinot noir producers in a very short period of time. The French term 'massale' describes a Burgundian wine that is a melange of all the clones on a property: so at Kooyong this is a blend of the 10 clones of pinot that they grow. It's second vintage (2003 was terrific too) of their entry level pinot: intense, aromatic, juicy raspberry, mulberry flavours, silky texture, good depth and length. Impressive and excellent value.

2003 Little Brother Shiraz Cabernet $16

This is a new second label for Zarephath, a small vineyard in the Porongurups run by the religious community of Christ Circle. As you would remember, in the Book of Kings, Zarephath was the place where Elijah found sustenance after he had fled from Queen Jezebel. Christ Circle was originally from California and came to Albany by boat after many adventures and misadventures. They are engaged in several enterprises and have turned their hand to viticulture with a deal of success. (Here endeth the sermon.) The wines are made by Rob Diletti at nearby Castle Rock. Little Brother is cleverly marketed with a catchy label – something of a rarity in the Porongurups. This 2003 Shiraz Cabernet has attractive sweet, dark berry fruit, smooth texture, a pleasing succulent mouthfeel and a gentle supple finish. The 2004 Little Brother Unwooded Chardonnay is also recommended.

2002 Majella Cabernet Sauvignon $30

An impressive Coonawarra cabernet from one of the region's hottest and most consistent producers: lovely sweet berry fragrance, complex blackberry, blueberry and chocolate flavours and fine slinky tannins. Good drinking now and over the next five years.

2004 Majella 'The Musician' Cabernet Shiraz $18

A tribute by his family to a talented young musician, Matthew Lynn, who was killed in a hit-and-run incident late last year. Arguably the best red currently available at this price point. A delicious, approachable Coonawarra cabernet shiraz blend that is vibrant, fruit-driven (raspberries, mulberries, blackcurrants) with depth of flavour and a gentle, lingering finish.

2001 Minot Cabernet Sauvignon $28

This is a robust, powerful red from a new-ish Margaret River producer that has attractive cassis and mulberry flavours with noticeable cedary oak, velvety texture and deep, ripe tannins.

2004 Mr Riggs Shiraz Viognier $25

This McLaren Vale producer is making one of the most consistent and best-value shiraz viognier blends in the country. The 2004 is smooth and approachable, fruit-driven yet with good depth of ripe, dark berry flavours and a balanced finish that lingers.

2002 Nugan Estate Shiraz $23.95

While this is at the upper end of what you would expect to pay for a Riverina red, it is well worth the money. There's more depth, richness and concentration than we are used to seeing from the region: it's generous, bright and vibrant.

2003 O'Leary Walker Shiraz $22

This is a blend from the Clare and McLaren Vale: restrained, brooding, dense blackcurrant flavours, smooth texture and an extractive finish that remains approachable. Will improve with a bit more time in the bottle. Good value.

2001 Pauletts Shiraz $22

There is a print in my office showing what I regard as the most stunning wine country scene in Australia: the view from Clare Valley winery Pauletts looking over the Polish Hill River Valley. The Pauletts wines are pretty smart too: this has ripe redcurrant and garden herb flavours, smooth, fleshy texture and a fine, gentle finish.

2001 Potters Clay Shiraz $16.95

It's quite a common story these days, especially in South Australia – a new-ish label from an established grape-growing family. This is a well-priced McLaren Vale shiraz that is soft, round and very easy-drinking – lots of vanilla bean for those who enjoy oak.

2003 Punt Road Merlot $25

Another good Yarra Valley varietal from winemaker Kate Goodman: ripe plummy flavours, fleshy texture, tight structure, and a pleasing grip to finish. Will improve in the short term but it's approachable now.

2002 Redbank 'Fighting Flat' Shiraz $21

The Pyrenees winery's move to source fruit from the King Valley is once again paying off with this impressive shiraz: attractive vanillin oak flavours are obvious but there's enough ripe powerful fruit to provide balance; texture is smooth; satisfying and approachable now.

2003 Rockbare Shiraz $20

This is a new McLaren Vale producer who is making determined inroads into a tough marketplace thanks to wines such as this attractive shiraz: cedary oak, ripe blackberries, smooth texture. Made for immediate and easy drinking.

2003 Saint Clair Pinot Noir $23

There are some very good, easy-drinking Kiwi pinots at about this price point including the Saint Clair with its light to medium body, smooth texture, ripe, rich flavours and good varietal character. A pleasant drink.

2003 St Hallett 'Blackwell' Shiraz $29.50

By comparison with the Barossa super-premium shiraz, this is extraordinarily good value for money from one of the Valley's most reliable shiraz producers: floral nose, rich, concentrated plummy flavours, fine, ripe tannins. Harmonious, balanced, fine and generous.

2002 Saltram 'Next Chapter' Cabernet Merlot $16

This Saltram red is better than most cabernet merlots in this price bracket and it continues the fine run that this label has had with their reds in the past few years. Unless I'm given some help, I can't for the life of me remember the new Saltram labels – Marker's Table varietals ($8–$10); Next Chapter ($14–$16), Saltram's mid-price range of wines from the Barossa Valley – and I think the names are quite silly. Fortunately, the wines are pretty good. The 2002 Saltram 'Next Chapter' has ripe redcurrant flavours, smooth texture and reasonable balance. With a hearty beef casserole, it'll make a good drink.

2002 Scarpantoni 'Block 3' Shiraz $22

From a well-established, traditional McLaren Vale producer who has fashioned a powerful, deeply flavoured, richly concentrated shiraz that will improve with some age. Excellent value – and I'd be happy to enjoy it now.

2003 Seppelt 'Chalambar' Shiraz $23.95

For many years, this has been one of the best value reds in the country. Although the price is creeping up, it's still a very impressive red – and, it must be said, still very good value. There may be some 2002 around – dried herb aromas, soft, fleshy texture, good richness and concentration – but the 2003 is even better – spicy, succulent, big, ripe, sweet red berry fruit, lush and smooth texture before substantial fine tannins and a long, dry finish. It will improve with short term cellaring.

2003 Seppelt 'Victoria' Cabernet Sauvignon $16.95
2003 Seppelt 'Victoria' Shiraz $16.95

With a base in the Barossa – now the focus of its superb fortifieds – and another at Great Western, Seppelt has sometimes struggled with its identity. In recent years, it has been making outstanding shiraz from the Grampians and has worked hard to develop its Victorian focus. I can't remember a better pair of reds under its Victorian label than the Shiraz and Cabernet Sauvignon from the 2003 vintage. With both having a recommended retail of $16.95 and often selling for under $15, these are quaffing bargains. The 2003 Seppelt 'Victoria' Shiraz has dense, concentrated, rich dark plum, anise and chocolate flavours, is smooth and approachable, and finishes with ripe, sweet tannins. Delicious! The 2003 Seppelt 'Victoria' Cabernet is more restrained, with deep, dark berry fruit, heaps of cedary oak giving power and density. It's tight and firmer and needs some time: a bit like the difference between shiraz and cabernet really.

2004 Six Foot Six Pinot Noir $16

Arguably the best Australian pinot noir under $20 currently on the market, from a long-established Geelong producer, Austin's Barrabool, which has significantly increased production in recent years. It is gently fragrant, supple, almost silky, with good varietal character in the red cherry, strawberry spectrum, light-bodied but reasonably intense.

2003 Skuttlebutt Cabernet Shiraz Merlot $17.50

From the folks that gave us Suckfizzle and Stella Bella, comes an imaginative budget-priced label that delivers quality wine at a fair price. Smooth, ripe, red berry flavours – an unpretentious quaffer.

2004 Tamar Ridge 'Devil's Corner' Pinot Noir $17.95

Now owned by Tasmanian timber company Gunns, and rapidly expanding at present, Tamar Ridge has stuck to its original character of producing good Tassie wines at affordable prices. This has attractive varietal character – red berries, red cherries – and is smooth with a strong tannin backbone – so it's a little heavy on the finish.

2003 Tinja Sangiovese Merlot $18

This is one of the labels of David Lowe and Jane Wilson – now based in Mudgee. The address is Tinja Lane in case you, too, wondered about the name. This is a straightforward red blend (after the Tuscan model): attractive cedary oak aromas, juicy red berry fruit with some savoury notes and a soft, easy finish.

2004 Torbreck Woodcutters Red $20

David Powell's Barossa winery Torbreck makes all of its red wines using a traditional basket press, which must be a time-consuming pain in the neck since the volumes it produces have soared (largely as a result of the success of this Barossa shiraz). The 2003 marked a leap in quality, which this vintage continues. It is nicely fragrant, has ripe plummy fruit with a hint of brambles, smooth texture and fine, soft tannins. Best of all, it is made to be drunk young and so is approachable now.

2002 Tyrrells 'Rufus Stone' Heathcote Shiraz $22

Economies of scale enable Tyrrells to sell this at prices way below the norm for one of Australia's hottest new shiraz regions. It's robust and powerfully flavoured so the substantial, quality fruit balances the strong oak and tannins. Impressive.

2003 Voyager Estate Shiraz $29.50

Trophy winner at last year's Margaret River Show and another sign that the Voyager reds have come of age. Complex, white pepper and vanilla bean aromas, ultra-smooth texture, intense black berry flavours, approachable and enticing. You won't get better value from Margaret River.

2003 Wolf Blass 'Gold Label' Cabernet Sauvignon Cabernet Franc $22
2003 Wolf Blass 'Gold Label' Shiraz Viognier $22

Here are two additions to Wolf Blass' popular Gold Label range, which is doing better than ever at this price point. The Adelaide Hills cabernet blend has attractive cedary oak, blackberry and mulberry flavours, a firm structure and a powerful finish. On the other hand, the Shiraz Viognier has more fleshy texture and ripe dark plum flavours, which are well-integrated with spicy oak. Approachable now.

2003 Woodlands Cabernet Merlot $20

Woodlands is one of Margaret River's pioneering vineyards (planted in 1973) and lies adjacent to Brookland Valley and over the road from Moss Wood. Its potential has been limited because it has been a part-time operation. With full-time attention from Stuart, son of founders David and Heather Watson, Woodlands is undergoing rejuvenation and making some excellent wines. This is a surprise packet as it's from vines planted in 1998 but has much greater concentration and depth than you'd expect. The 2003 Woodlands Cabernet Merlot has dense cassis and cedary oak flavours, amazing power, smooth texture and fine ripe tannins. It is quite oaky and extractive so if you like the style, this is a very well-priced, young Margaret River red. Only $16.50 from cellar door.

2003 Yangarra Grenache Shiraz Mourvedre $28

The giant Californian winemaker Kendal Jackson bought into McLaren Vale by buying the old Normans vineyard, which they use to obtain fruit for this wine. I confess that I loved both the 2003 and 2002 vintages: it's just so wonderfully drinkable – 'whooshable' as one of my pals says. It has density of red berry flavour, is rich, concentrated and powerful, yet is so lush and fleshy that it is not just approachable, it's inviting.

Sweet and Fortified Wines over $15

SWEET WINES

2004 Bethany 'Select' Late Harvest Riesling (500ml) $18

The Schrapel family's Barossa winery is featured regularly in *Quaff* with its stickies. This has some apricot and marmalade flavours, pleasing sweetness and cleansing lemony acidity.

2004 T'Gallant Moscato $20

This Mornington Peninsula producer may be owned by Beringer Blass, but it continues to make wines just as it did while family-owned. The fruit for this wine comes from Swan Hill and shows what this area can do with appropriate grape varieties. There are seductive grapey aromas, a slight salmon-pink tinge, grapey, muscaty flavours, and a gentle sweet zing on a refreshing finish.

FORTIFIED WINES

All Saints Rutherglen Muscat $19

There are four levels of muscat from this region: Rutherglen, Classic, Grand and Rare (in ascending order of richness, concentration and power). The bargains are often to be found in this price bracket. This is fragrant, direct and focused with clear raisiny varietal characters. Sweeter than some.

All Saints Rutherglen Tokay $19

While this doesn't have concentration or depth – you wouldn't expect that – it is fine, intense but lightly framed with sweet, lush malt, toffee and butterscotch flavours.

Baileys 'Founder' Port $20

A surprise packet: soft, round and easy-drinking, yet with richness and concentration and deceptive layer after layer of barley sugar, molasses and toffee flavours. Fine, intense, balanced and cheap.

Brown Brothers Reserve Muscat $18.50

A well-priced fortified from this popular family company based in north-eastern Victoria: lush raisiny flavours, sweet, soft and approachable.

Buller Fine Old Tokay $20

Another bargain from a long-established Rutherglen family. This is deep and opulent with malt, toffee, butter-scotch and treacle flavours and has quite a strong, spirity finish.

Campbells Rutherglen Muscat $18.35

The Campbell family have been making these great forti-fieds in this part of the world for more than 130 years – and it shows in the wines. This has impressive depth and concentration, has sweet raisiny flavours, lush texture and a dryish finish that lingers.

1997 Hardys Vintage Port $25.95

I enjoyed this wine in the tasting. And somehow, I couldn't resist having a sip or two at the end of a hard winter's day. Same thing happened the next evening ... and so on. It has liquorice, anise and blackcurrant flavours, lush, ripe, sweet fruit and a gentle, lingering finish. In a word: 'gulpa-ble'. It's a bit expensive but you do get 750 ml, which goes a long way with a fortified.

Morris Liqueur Tokay $16.95

They used to rave about what a great fortified winemaker Mick Morris was. It must be in the genes because his son David has continued the family tradition and is, in my view, the greatest maker of muscats and tokays in the country. Sure, he's helped by the fact that he has fantastic resources of aged fortifieds safely hidden in barrels at the Rutherglen winery. I've just tasted more than 70 muscats, tokays, tawnies and other fortifieds at all price points (not in the one sitting). They are magnificent and offer fantastic value. But the star of the show was unquestionably David Morris. This liqueur tokay is my pick of the fortifieds under $25. While I may be bowled over by the power and concentration of the aged tokays, they are so rich that there are limits to how much you can guzzle. This fresh, light, sweet fortified is a different – and slightly dangerous – story. It's wonderfully fragrant, has honeyed, butterscotch, malt and toffee flavours and finishes with refreshing acidity that prevents it from being cloying. A great way to finish an evening. A bargain.

Seppelt DP 57 Grand Tokay $26.95

One of the great bargains: a Rutherglen tokay from this Barossa-based large company. It has enormous depth, weight and density of flavour (caramel, malt and toffee) as well as impeccable balance. It is unctuous, sweet, velvety, long and fine.

Seppelt Para 123 Liqueur Tawny $18.95

A beautifully balanced tawny with malt, butterscotch and toffee flavours and a fine gentle finish.

How to track down the bargains

HOW AND WHERE TO BUY GREAT-VALUE WINE

If you're really keen on finding bargains in bottleshop land, one of the best things you can do is make a nuisance of yourself – in the nicest possible way, of course. Make sure the people behind the counter at your favourite wine emporium know you're interested in drinking good grog, and are looking out for bargains. If they're doing their job properly, they should nurture you as a valued customer – you buying cheap wine on a regular basis is just as important as one-off sales of expensive booze to people who'll never come back.

As a wine consumer, you have two choices. You can sit back and let the wine shops seduce you into buying this week's unbeatable special through their advertising and their promotions and their smooth talking. Or you can make a little bit of effort and discover your own specials all by yourself. Here are a few tips to help you become a well-informed, quick-thinking, quick-quaffing wine bargain explorer.

Some Tips for the Bargain Hunter

Read about wine

Yeah, I know the old saying, 'don't believe everything you read', but in the cause of finding good-value wine, I reckon you should take notice of at least some of the many thousands of words published about wine in newspapers, magazines and over the internet each week. Gaining knowledge about how wines are made, where they come from, why they taste different, and what foods go well with them, will help you become a more discerning customer.

Quaff online at is a great source of wine information and reviews, and the best way to keep your copy of *Quaff* up to date throughout the year. **To receive weekly reviews of great-value wines, subscribe for FREE at www.quaff.com.au.** We'll let you know as soon as the best new wines under $15 hit the market. Don't forget to tell your friends, and *Quaff* on!

Buy up big

In the short term, buying wines by the case, or dozen bottles, can be a real pain in the back pocket. But I thoroughly recommend it, as you are almost guaranteed to receive a discount. If you can't afford it yourself, get together with a group of mates and each chip in the cost of a couple of bottles – that way you spread the cost but share the benefits.

See Australia now

No amount of reading beats experience. Most Australians live a few hours' drive from a wine region. There's no excuse then, not to get into the car and visit a couple of cellar doors. Here you'll (hopefully) get an idea of how to taste wine for maximum enjoyment, and you'll be able to (hopefully) learn about how grapes are grown. Cellar doors are also great places to find discounted wines – bargain bins, ends of vintage, reduced to clear, often on tasting before you buy. Many wineries have mailing lists that you can join, and offer exclusive bargains to mailing list members. If you can't visit a cellar door, then many wine shops have in-store tastings, and wine exhibitions are enjoying increasing popularity.

Spend more money

You probably don't expect to be told this in a book dedicated to finding the most enjoyment for the least expense, but a big tip is to try and spend a little bit more on wine than you did last time (within reason, of course, and without plunging yourself into debt ... although I can talk). If you're used to spending $6, try a $9.95 bottle of the same variety or style next time you visit the bottleshop; if $10 is your usual spend, lash out on a $15 bottle – and so on. Another idea is to buy these slightly more expensive bottles once a week for a special Friday or Saturday dinner or a long Sunday lunch with friends. You may very well think that the extra money isn't worth it – in which case, revert to the old favourites and save yourself some cash. But you may also find that the slightly pricier wines can offer better value for money – in other words, by increasing your spend by 20 per cent, you can increase your enjoyment by 100 per cent. You won't know, though, unless you try for yourself.

Don't believe the hype

Be very careful out there. Australian wine marketing departments are
incredibly clever at attaching little shiny round stickers to their labels
that look uncannily like medals won at some wine show or other.
Don't be fooled. Read the shiny stickers carefully. If they tell you the
wine has won two bronze medals, it means it was judged to be fair to
average quality on two separate occasions. If they tell you the winery
was judged Winery of the Year at some international drinks fair in
Finland in 1986, be cautious. And even if they tell you that the wine in
the bottle has won a string of gold medals and trophies, while you can
be safe that the wine is well-made, that's no guarantee you will like it.
Again – and again, again – try before you buy, if you can.

Finding the Wines

This index will enable you to source further information on any of the wines reviewed in *Quaff*, such as your nearest local stockist. The name by which the wine is known (the winery or label) is followed by the name of the distributor (where appropriate), a website or email address (in all but one case) and a contact number.

ALKOOMI
www.alkoomiwines.com.au   (08) 9855 2229

ALL SAINTS
www.allsaintswine.com.au   1800 021 621

ANDREW GARRETT
www.andrewgarrett.com.au   (08) 8334 2000

ANGOVE'S
www.angoves.com.au   (08) 8580 3100

ANGUS
www.anguswines.com.au   (08) 8555 2320

ANNIE'S LANE (Beringer Blass)
www.beringerblass.com.au   (03) 8626 3300

ARAKOON
www.arakoonwine.com   (08) 8323 7339

AUSTRALIAN OLD VINE
sales@.australianoldvine.com.au   (02) 6963 5239

BAILEYS (Beringer Blass)
www.beringerblass.com.au   (03) 8626 3300

BALDIVIS ESTATE (Palandri)
www.palandri.com.au   (08) 9216 7000

BALNAVES
www.balnaves.com.au   (08) 8737 2946

BANROCK STATION (Hardy Wine Company)
www.hardywines.com.au   (02) 9666 5855

BARKING OWL (Millbrook)
www.millbrookwinery.com.au   (08) 9525 5796

BARRECAS
barreca@bigpond.com.au   (08) 9731 1716

BARWANG (McWilliams)
www.mcwilliams.com.au   1800 800 584

BARWICK ESTATE
www.barwickwines.com (08) 9755 7100

BAY OF FIRES (Hardy Wine Company)
www.hardywines.com.au (02) 9666 5855

BEELGARA ESTATE
www.beelgaraestate.com.au (02) 6966 0288

BERESFORD
www.beresfordwines.com.au (08) 8323 8899

BETHANY
www.bethany.com.au (08) 8563 2086

BIMBADGEN
www.bimbadgen.com.au (02) 4998 7585

BLEASDALE
www.bleasdale.com.au (08) 8537 3001

BLUE PYRENEES
www.bluepyrenees.com.au (02) 9387 4299

BLUES POINT (Southcorp)
www.southcorpwines.com (02) 9465 1000

BOWEN ESTATE (Tucker Seabrook)
www.tuckerseabrook.com.au (02) 9666 0033

BRANDS (McWilliams)
www.mcwilliams.com.au 1800 800 584

BROKEN EARTH (Tandou)
www.tandou.com.au (08) 8583 6500

BROOMSTICK
www.broomstick.com.au (08) 9271 9594

BROWN BROTHERS
www.brown-brothers.com.au (03) 5720 5500

BROWNS OF PADTHAWAY
www.browns-of-padthaway.com (08) 8765 6040

BUCKLAND GAP (Victorian Alps)
www.victorianalpswinery.com (03) 5751 1199

BULLER
www.buller.com.au (02) 6032 9660

CAMPBELLS
www.campbellswine.com.au (02) 6032 9458

CAPE MENTELLE
www.capementelle.com.au (08) 9757 0888

CAPE SCHANCK (Beringer Blass)
www.beringerblass.com.au   (03) 8626 3300

CAPEL VALE
www.capelvale.com   (08) 9727 0105

CARRINGTON (Orlando)
www.orlandowyndhamgroup.com   (08) 8208 2444

CARTWHEEL (Beringer Blass)
www.beringerblass.com.au   (03) 8626 3300

CASTELLO DI GABBIANO (Beringer Blass)
www.beringerblass.com.au   (03) 8626 3300

CERRO DEL MASSO (Prince Wine Store)
www.princewinestor.com.au   (03) 9536 1155

CHAIN OF PONDS
www.chainofponds.com.au   (08) 8389 1415

CHANNYBEARUP
www.channybearup.com.au   (08) 9480 2000

CHAPOUTIER
www.mchapoutieraustralia.com   (03) 9429 8301

CHARLES MELTON
www.charlesmeltonwines.com.au   (08) 8563 3606

CHATEAU TANUNDA
www.chateautanunda.com   (08) 8563 3888

CHESTNUT GROVE
www.awl.com.au   (08) 9368 0099

CHEVIOT BRIDGE
www.cheviotbridge.com.au   (03) 9820 9080

CHIVITE (Trembath &Taylor)
virginia@trembathandtaylor.com.au   (03) 9696 7018

CHRISMONT
www.chrismont.com.au   (03) 5729 8220

CLOVELY
www.clovely.com.au   (07) 3216 1088

COCKATOO RIDGE (Tucker Seabrook)
www.tuckerseabrook.com.au   (02) 9666 0033

COLDSTREAM HILLS (Southcorp)
www.southcorpwines.com   (02) 9465 1000

COOKOOTHAMA (Nugan Estate)
tnugan@nuganestate.com.au   (02) 6962 1822

COOLABAH (Orlando)
www.orlandowyndhamgroup.com   (08) 8208 2444

CORA (Vintage Cellars)
www.vintagecellars.com.au   1300 366 084

CORIOLE
www.coriole.com   (08) 8323 8305

COWRA ESTATE
cowraestate@ozemail.com.au   (02) 6342 1136

CROCODILE CREEK (Trembath &Taylor)
virginia@trembathandtaylor.com.au   (03) 9696 7018

CROFTERS (Hardy Wine Company)
www.hardywines.com.au   (02) 9666 5855

CUMULUS
www.cumuluswines.com.au   (02) 6390 7900

D'ARENBERG
www.darenberg.com.au   1800 882 335

DAL BROI
info@dalbroiwines.com.au   (02) 6953 0855

DE BORTOLI
www.debortoli.com.au   (02) 9636 6033

DEAKIN ESTATE
www.deakinestate.com.au   (03) 5029 1666

DEUTZ (Montana)
www.montanawines.co.au   (02) 8878 6000

DOWIE DOOLE
www.dowiedoole.com   (08) 8323 7428

ELDERTON
www.eldertonwines.com.au   (08) 8568 7878

EVANS & TATE
www.evansandtate.com.au   (08) 6462 1799

FERNGROVE
www.ferngrove.com.au   (08) 9227 0297

FIDDLERS CREEK (Blue Pyrenees)
www.bluepyrenees.com.au   (02) 9387 4299

FISHBONE (Blackwood)
www.fishbonewines.com   (08) 9756 0088

FISHER'S CIRCLE (Southcorp)
www.southcorpwines.com   (02) 9465 1000

FLYING FISH COVE
www.flyingfishcove.com   (08) 9755 6600

FOUR SISTERS (Tahbilk)
www.tahbilk.com.au   (03) 5794 2555

FOX CREEK
www.foxcreekwines.com   (08) 8556 2403

FOX RIVER (Goundrey)
www.goundreywines.com.au   (08) 9366 3900

GALAH (Ashton Hills)
ashtonhills@bigpond.com   (08) 8390 1243

GAPSTED
www.gapstedwines.com   (03) 5751 1383

GEMTREE
www.gemtreevineyards.com.au   (08) 8323 8199

GEOFF MERRILL
www.geoffmerrillwines.com   (08) 8381 6877

GILBERTS
email: gilberts@rainbow.agn.net.au   (08) 9851 4028

GLAETZER
www.glaetzer.com   (08) 8563 0288

GOUNDREY
www.goundreywines.com.au   (08) 9366 3900

GRAMPS (Orlando)
www.orlandowyndhamgroup.com   (08) 8208 2444

GRANDIN (Tucker Seabrook)
www.tuckerseabrook.com.au   (02) 9666 0033

HAMILTON'S EWELL
www.hamiltonewell.com.au   (08) 8231 0088

HARDYS (Hardy Wine Company)
www.hardywines.com.au   (02) 9666 5855

HASELGROVE (Vintage Cellars)
www.vintagecellars.com.au   1300 366 084

HAZARD HILL (Plantagenet)
www.plantagenetwines.com   (08) 9851 3111

HEARTLAND
www.heartlandwines.com.au   (08) 8357 9344

HEEMSKERK (Cellarmasters)
www.cellarmasters.com.au   1800 500 260

HENRY FESSY (Vintage Cellars)
www.vintagecellars.com.au 1300 366 084

HERITAGE
herwine@ozemail.com.au (08) 8562 2880

HOUGHTON (Hardy Wine Company)
www.hardywines.com.au (02) 9666 5855

JACOBS CREEK (Orlando)
www.orlandowyndhamgroup.com (08) 8208 2444

JAMIESONS RUN (Beringer Blass)
www.beringerblass.com.au (03) 8626 3300

JANE BROOK
www.janebrook.com.au (08) 9274 1432

JIM BARRY
jbwines@jimbarry.com (08) 8842 2261

JINGALLA
www.jingallawines.com.au (08) 9853 1023

JIP JIP ROCKS (Morambro Creek)
mcwine@rbm.com.au (08) 8765 6043

JUNIPER CROSSING (Juniper Estate)
www.juniperestate.com.au (08) 9451 7277

KAISER STUHL (Southcorp)
www.southcorpwines.com (02) 9465 1000

KANGAROO RIDGE (Cowra Estate)
cowraestate@ozemail.com.au (02) 6342 1136

KILIKANOON
www.kilikanoon.com.au (08) 8843 4377

KINGSTON ESTATE
www.kingstonestatewines.com (08) 8130 4500

KIRRIHILL ESTATES
www.kirrihillestates.com.au (08) 8842 1233

KNAPPSTEIN (Lion Nathan)
www.knappstein.com.au (08) 8842 2600

KOOYONG
www.kooyong.com (08) 8112 4210

LA BELLE TERRASSE (Southcorp)
www.southcorpwines.com (02) 9465 1000

LA VIEILLE FERME (Negociants)
www.negociants.com (08) 8561 3200

LEAPING LIZARD (Ferngrove)
www.ferngrove.com.au   (08) 9227 0297

LEASINGHAM (Hardy Wine Company)
www.hardywines.com.au   (02) 9666 5855

LILLYDALE (McWilliams)
www.mcwilliams.com.au   1800 800 584

LILLYPILLY
www.lillypilly.com   (02) 6953 4069

LILYVALE
www.lilyvalewines.com   (07) 4653 5280

LINDAUER (Montana)
www.montanawines.co.au   (02) 8878 6000

LINDEMANS (Southcorp)
www.southcorpwines.com   (02) 9465 1000

LION NATHAN
www.lion-nathan.com.au   1800 308 388

LITTLE BROTHER (Zarephath)
www.zarephathwines.com   (08) 9853 1152

LITTLE PENGUIN (Southcorp)
www.southcorpwines.com   (02) 9465 1000

LOGAN
www.loganwines.com.au   (02) 6373 1333

LONG FLAT WINE COMPANY (Cheviot Bridge)
www.cheviotbridge.com.au   (03) 9820 9080

MADFISH
www.madfishwines.com.au   (08) 9423 1200

MAJELLA
www.majellawines.com.au   (08) 8736 3055

MASI (Red+White)
www.redandwhite.com.au   (03) 8413 8310

MATTHEW LANG (Southcorp)
www.southcorpwines.com   (02) 9465 1000

McGUIGAN (Icon Brands)
www.mcguiganwines.co.au   (02) 8345 6377

McPHERSON
www.mcphersonwines.com   02 9436 1644

McWILLIAMS
www.mcwilliams.com.au   1800 800 584

MILDARA (Beringer Blass)
www.beringerblass.com.au   (03) 8626 3300

MINCHINBURY (Southcorp)
www.southcorpwines.com   (02) 9465 1000

MINOT
minot@wn.com.au   (08) 9757 3579

MISTLETOE
www.mistletoe.com.au   1800 055 080

MITCHELTON (Lion Nathan)
www.mitchelton.com.au   (03) 5736 2222

MONDORO (McWilliams)
www.mcwilliams.com.au   1800 800 584

MONTANA
www.montanawines.com.au   (02) 8878 6000

MOONDAH BROOK (Hardy Wine Company)
www.hardywines.com.au   (02) 9666 5855

MORAMBRO CREEK
mcwines@rbm.com.au   (08) 8765 6043

MORRIS (Orlando)
www.orlandowyndhamgroup.com   (08) 8208 2444

MOUNT MAJURA
www.mountmajura.com.au   (02) 6262 3070

MOUNT PLEASANT (McWilliams)
www.mcwilliams.com.au   1800 800 584

MOUNT RILEY (Angove's)
www.angoves.com.au   (08) 8580 3100

MR RIGGS
mrriggs@pennyshill.com.au   (08) 8556 4460

MT TRIO
mttrio@omninet.net.au   (08) 9853 1136

NEPENTHE
www.nepenthe.com.au   (08) 8398 8888

NINTH ISLAND (Pipers Brook)
www.pipersbrook.com   (03) 6332 4444

NORMANNO (Enoteca Sileno)
alladmin@enoteca.com.au   (03) 9347 5044

NOVA (Westend Estate)
www.westendestate.com   (02) 6964 1506

NUGAN ESTATE
tnugan@nuganestate.com.au   (02) 6962 1822

O'LEARY WALKER
www.olearywalkerwines.com   (08) 8843 0022

OMNI (Hardy Wine Company)
www.hardywines.com.au   (02) 9666 5855

OYSTER BAY
www.oysterbaywines.com.au   (02) 9317 9800

PALANDRI
www.palandri.com.au   (08) 9216 7000

PARRI
www.parriestate.com.au   (08) 8554 9595

PAUL CONTI
www.paulcontiwines.com.au   (08) 9409 9160

PAULETT
paulwine@rbe.net.au   (08) 8843 4328

PENFOLDS (Southcorp)
www.southcorpwines.com   (02) 9465 1000

PEPPERJACK (Beringer Blass)
www.beringerblass.com.au   (03) 8626 3300

PERTARINGA
www.pertaringa.com.au   (08) 8323 8125

PETALUMA (Lion Nathan)
www.petaluma.com.au   1300 780 735

PETER LEHMANN
www.peterlehmannwines.com.au   (08) 8843 4370

PEWSEY VALE (Yalumba)
www.yalumba.com   (08) 8112 4200

PIKES (Tucker Seabrook)
www.tuckerseabrook.com.au   (02) 9666 0033

PILLAR BOX RED (Henry's Drive)
www.henrysdrive.com   (08) 8765 5251

PITCHFORK (Hay Shed Hill)
www.hayshedhill.com.au   (08) 9368 0099

POETS CORNER (Orlando)
www.orlandowyndhamgroup.com   (08) 8208 2444

POTTERS CLAY	(08) 8556 2799
PRIMO ESTATE	
www.primoestate.com.au	(08) 8380 9442
PRUNOTTO (Negociants)	
www.negociants.com	(08) 8561 3200
PUMP HILL (Roberts Estate)	
www.robertsestatewines.com	(03) 5024 5704
PUNT ROAD	
www.puntroadwines.com.au	(03) 9739 0666
QUEEN ADELAIDE (Southcorp)	
www.southcorpwines.com	(02) 9465 1000
RALLO (Enoteca Sileno)	
alladmin@enoteca.com.au	(03) 9347 5044
RED DEER STATION (Dal Broi)	
info@dalbroiwines.com.au	(02) 6953 0855
REDBANK	
www.sallyspaddock.com.au	(03) 5467 7255
RICCADONNA (Southcorp)	
www.southcorpwines.com	(02) 9465 1000
RICHMOND GROVE (Orlando)	
www.orlandowyndhamgroup.com	(08) 8208 2444
ROBERTS ESTATE	
www.robertsestatewines.com	(03) 5024 5704
ROCKBARE	
www.rockbare.com.au	(08) 8389 9584
ROCKFIELD	
www.rockfield.com.au	(08) 9757 5006
ROSEMOUNT ESTATE (Southcorp)	
www.southcorpwines.com	(02) 9465 1000
ROSSETTO (Beelgara Estate)	
www.beelgaraestate.com.au	(02) 6966 0288
ROUGE HOMME (Southcorp)	
www.southcorpwines.com	(02) 9465 1000
RUFFINO (Vintage Cellars)	
www.vintagecellars.com.au	1300 366 084
RUTHERGLEN ESTATES	
cellar@rutherglenestates.com.au	(02) 6032 8516

SAINT CLAIR (MGM Distributors)
info@mgmwines.com.au   (08) 9244 3299

SALISBURY (Evans & Tate)
www.evansandtate.com.au   (08) 9213 1799

SALTRAM (Beringer Blass)
www.beringerblass.com.au   (03) 8626 330

SANDALFORD
www.sandalford.com   (08) 9374 9374

SARANTOS (Kingston Estate)
www.kingstonestatewines.com   (08) 8130 4500

SCARPANTONI
www.scarpontoni-wines.com.au   (08) 8383 0186

SCHILD ESTATE
www.schildestate.com.au   (08) 8524 5560

SELAKS (Vintage Cellars)
www.vintagecellars.com.au   1300 366 084

SEPPELT (Southcorp)
www.southcorpwines.com   (02) 9465 1000

SIEGERSDORF (Hardy Wine Company)
www.hardywines.com.au   (02) 9666 5855

SIMON GILBERT
www.simongilbertwines.com.au   (02) 6373 1245

SIR JAMES (Hardy Wine Company)
www.hardywines.com.au   (02) 9666 5855

SIRROMET
www.sirromet.com   (07) 3206 2999

SIX FOOT SIX (Austins Barrabool)
www.abwines.com.au   (03) 5281 1799

SKILLOGALEE
www.skillogalee.com.au   (08) 8843 4311

SKUTTLEBUTT (Stella Bella)
www.stellabella.com.au   (08) 9757 6377

SNOWY CREEK (Victorian Alps)
www.victorianalpswinery.com   (03) 5751 1992

SOLO ARTE (Arquilla)
www.arquilla.com   (02) 9560 9733

ST HALLETT (Lion Nathan)
www.sthallett.com.au   (08) 8563 7000

STICKS
www.sticks.com.au   (03) 9739 0666

STONEHAVEN (Hardy Wine Company)
www.hardywines.com.au   (02) 9666 5855

STONELEIGH (Montana)
www.montanawines.co.au   (02) 8878 6000

STONES (Angove's)
www.angoves.com.au   (08) 8580 3100

T'GALLANT (Beringer Blass)
www.beringerblass.com.au   (03) 8626 3300

TAHBILK
www.tahbilk.com.au   (03) 5794 2555

TALL POPPY
www.tallpoppywines.com   (03) 5022 7255

TAMAR RIDGE
www.tamarridgewines.com.au   (03) 6394 1111

TANDOU
www.tandou.com.au   (08) 8583 6500

TAYLORS
www.taylorswines.com.au   (08) 8849 2008

TEMPUS TWO
www.temputwo.com.au   (02) 4993 3999

TERRA FELIX (Tallarook)
www.terrafelix.com.au   (03) 9876 7022

TINJA (Lowe Family)
www.lowewine.com.au   (02) 6372 2855

TOBACCO ROAD (Victorian Alps)
www.victorianalpswinery.com   (03) 5751 1992

TOLLANA (Southcorp)
www.southcorpwines.com   (02) 9465 1000

TORBRECK
www.torbreck.com   (08) 8562 4155

TORRES (Negociants)
www.negociants.com   (08) 8561 3200

TORZI MATTHEWS
wineevol@bigpond.net.au   (02) 9327 4609

TOSTI (Arquilla)
www.arquilla.com   (02) 9560 9733

TRENTHAM ESTATE
www.trenthamestate.com.au   (03) 5024 8888

TULLOCH (Angoves)
www.angoves.com.au   (08) 8580 3100

TURKEY FLAT
www.turkeyflat.com.au   (08) 8563 2851

TWIN ISLANDS (Yalumba)
www.yalumba.com   (08) 8112 4200

TWO HANDS
www.twohandswines.com   (08) 8367 0555

TYRRELLS
www.tyrrells.com.au   (02) 9889 4450

UMANI RONCHI (Trembath &Taylor)
virginia@trembathandtaylor.com.au   (03) 9696 7018

UPPER REACH
www.upperreach.com.au   (08) 9296 0078

VIDAL FLEURY (Vintage Cellars)
www.vintagecellars.com.au   1300 366 084

VINTAGE CELLARS
www.vintagecellars.com.au   1300 366 084

VOYAGER ESTATE
www.voyagerestate.com.au   (08) 9385 3133

WANGOLINA STATION
www.wangolinastation.com.au   (08) 8768 6187

WESTEND ESTATE
www.westendestate.com   (02) 6964 1506

WHITE ISLAND (Montana)
www.montanawines.com.au   (02) 8878 6000

WILDFLY (Channybearup)
www.channybearup.com.au   (08) 9480 2000

WIRRA WIRRA
www.wirrawirra.com   (08) 8112 4210

WOLF BLASS (Beringer Blass)
www.beringerblass.com.au   (03) 8626 3300

WOODLANDS
www.woodlands-wines.com.au   (08) 9755 6226

WOOP WOOP
www.woopwoop.com.au   (08) 8556 4460

WYNDHAM ESTATE (Orlando)
www.orlandowyndhamgroup.com   (08) 8208 2444

WYNNS (Southcorp)
www.southcorpwines.com   (02) 9465 1000

XABREGAS (Traolach)
www.traolach.com.au   1300 780 123

YALUMBA
www.yalumba.com   (08) 8112 4200

YANGARRA
www.yangarra.com   (08) 8383 7459

YELLOW TAIL (Casella)
www.casellawine.com.au   (02) 6961 3000

YERING STATION
www.yering.com   (03) 9730 0100

ZILZIE
www.zilziewines.com   (03) 5025 8100

ZONTE'S FOOTSTEP (Angas Vineyards)
angasvy@hotkey.net.au   (08) 8537 3337

Recommended Retailers

Again, making friends with a good bottleshop is the best way to gain direct access to the great bargains – the one-offs and specials as well as the wines from small producers that haven't yet become cult buys (and are therefore unobtainable). This list has been put together by combining our own experience of various bottleshops around the country, and asking a network of contacts, including wine producers, wholesalers and distributors, where the best places to buy wine are located.

NATIONAL

Because of their size (between them they control about 40 per cent of the market – and this percentage is growing), these stores often have the best prices, but they can lack range and depth of wines on offer.

Coles Myer – Liquorland, Vintage Cellars, Quaffers, Theo's

For store locations: 1300 366 084
www.vintagecellars.com.au

Woolworths – Safeway and Woolworths Liquor Stores, Dan Murphy's, BWS

For store locations: www.woolworths.com.au

NEW SOUTH WALES

SYDNEY

Amato's Liquor Mart

267 Norton Street, Leichhardt, NSW 2040
(02) 9560 7628

Annandale Cellars

119 Johnston Street, Annandale, NSW 2038
(02) 9660 1947

Avalon Fine Wine and Foods

35 Avalon Parade, Avalon, NSW 2107
(02) 9918 3207

Best Cellars

91 Crown Street, East Sydney, NSW 2010
(02) 9361 3733
www.bestcellars.com.au

Camperdown Cellars

140–144 Parramatta Road, Camperdown, NSW 2050
(02) 9517 2000

Cellarbrations

For store locations, contact state office:
Silverwater, 4 Newington Road, NSW 2264
(02) 9741 7231

Dee Why Hotel

Pittwater Road (cnr Sturdee Parade), Dee Why, NSW 2099
(02) 9981 1166

Five Way Cellars

4 Heeley Street, Paddington, NSW 2021
(02) 9360 4242

George's Liquor Nest

95 Willoughby Road, Crows Nest, NSW 2065
(02) 9437 6688

Jim's Cellars

65 Edgeworth David Avenue, Waitara, NSW 2077
(02) 9489 7177

Kemenys

137 Bondi Road, Bondi, 2026
13 88 81
www.kemenys.com.au

Liquor Brothers

3A Anella Avenue, Castle Hill, NSW 2154
(02) 9680 7311
www.liquorbrothers.com.au

Newport Bottler

386 Barrenjoey Road, Newport, NSW 2106
(02) 9997 6721

North Sydney Cellars
MLC Building, Shop 4, 105 Miller Street, North Sydney, NSW 2060
(02) 9954 0090
www.northsydneycellars.com.au

Palm Beach Wine Co.
1109 Barrenjoey Road, Palm Beach, 2108
(02) 9974 4304
www.palmbeachwineco.com

Polifroni Cellars
Shop 1, 169 Annangrove Road, Annangrove, NSW 2156
(02) 9679 0144

Porters Liquor
For store locations: www.portersliquor.com.au
(02) 9413 4800

OUTSIDE SYDNEY

Elanora Hotel
41 Victoria Street, Gosford East, NSW 2250
(02) 4325 2026
www.elanorahotel.com.au

Lambton Fridge
86 Elder Street, Lambton, NSW 2299
(02) 4957 1274

Leura Cellars
169–171 Leura Mall, Leura, NSW 2780
(02) 4784 1122

Oxford Tavern
47 Crown Street, Wollongong, NSW 2500
(02) 4228 3892

Toowoon Bay Cellars
153–155 Bay Road, Towoon Bay, NSW 2261
(02) 4332 7459

Tosti Cellars
Port Kembla, Wentworth Street, NSW 2505
(02) 4274 1315

VICTORIA

MELBOURNE

6J's Wine Merchants

Shop 814, Prahran Market, 163 Commercial Road,
South Yarra, VIC 3141
(03) 9824 2751
www.6jscleanskins.com.au

Armadale Cellars

813–817 High Street, Armadale, VIC 3143
(03) 9509 3055

City Wine Shop

159–161 Spring Street, Melbourne VIC 3000
(03) 9654 6657
www.citywineshop.net.au

Cloudwine Cellars

317 Clarendon Street, South Melbourne, VIC 3205
(03) 9699 6700
766 Burke Road, Camberwell, VIC 3124
(03) 9882 0954
www.cloudwine.com.au

Europa Cellars

Shop G3, Wellington Parade, East Melbourne VIC 3002
(03) 9417 7220

King & Godfree

293 Lygon Street, Carlton, VIC 3053
(03) 9347 1619
www.king&godfree.com.au

McCoppins

165 Johnston Street, Fitzroy, VIC 3065
(03) 9417 5089

Parkhill Cellars

43–45 Errol Street, North Melbourne, VIC 3051
(03) 9328 1132
www.parkhillcellars.com

Prince Wine Store

177 Bank Street, South Melbourne VIC 3205
(03) 9686 3033
2A Acland Street, St Kilda, VIC 3182
(03) 9536 1155
www.princewinestore.com.au

Randall The Wine Merchant

186 Bridport Street, Albert Park, VIC 3206
(03) 9686 4122
www.randalls.net.au

Rathdowne Cellars

348 Rathdowne Street, Carlton North, VIC 3054
(03) 9349 3366
www.rathdownecellars.com.au

Tannins Fine Wine

404 Queens Parade, Clifton Hill, VIC 3068
(03) 9482 2048

Winebins

58 Commercial Road, Prahran, VIC 3181
(03) 9510 5424
Outside Melbourne

OUTSIDE MELBOURNE

Bannockburn Cellars

150 Pakington Street, Geelong West, VIC 3218
(03) 5229 5358
www.bannockburncellars.com.au

Corky's Liquor

2–8 Breed Street, Traralgon, VIC 3844
(03) 5174 1211

Jack's Wine and Spirits

90 Sturt Street, Ballarat, VIC 3350
(03) 5332 1176
www.jackswine.com.au

K.M. Lynch

116 Fairy Street, Warrnambool, VIC 3280
(03) 5562 4939

Murray Esplanade Cellars

2 Leslie Street, Echuca, VIC 3564
(03) 5482 6058
mecellars@ozemail.com

Neuschafers

90 Mercer Street, Geelong, VIC 3220
(03) 5229 8871

Randall the Wine Merchant

324 Pakington Street, Newtown, VIC 2251
(03) 5223 1141
www.randalls.net.au

SOUTH AUSTRALIA

ADELAIDE

Cellarbrations

For store locations: 1800 650 880

East End Cellars

22–26 Vardon Avenue, Adelaide, SA 5000
(08) 8232 5300
www.eastendcellars.com.au

Edinburgh Cellars

7 High Street, Mitcham, SA 5062
(08) 8373 2700
www.edinburgh.com.au

Fassina Liquor Merchants

35 Oaklands Road, Somerton Park, SA 5044
(08) 8376 1848
admin@fassina.com.au

Goodwood Cellars

125 Goodwood Road, Goodwood SA 5034
(08) 8271 7481

Melbourne Street Cellars
93 Melbourne Street, North Adelaide, SA 5006
(08) 8267 1533

Norwood Hotel
97 The Parade, Norwood, SA 5067
(08) 8431 1822

Parade Cellars
Shop 15, 161–175 The Parade, Norwood SA 5067
(08) 8332 0317

Royal Oak Hotel
123 O'Connell Street, North Adelaide SA 5006
(08) 8267 2488

Wine Underground
121 Pirie Street, Adelaide, SA 5000
(08) 8232 1222
www.wineunderground.com.au

OUTSIDE ADELAIDE

Berri Resort Hotel
Riverview Drive, Berri, SA 5342
(08) 8582 1411
www.berriresorthotel.com

Fidler & Webb
64 Commercial Street East, Mount Gambier, SA 5290
(08) 8725 3038
fidwebb@datafast.net.au

Grand Tasman Hotel
94 Tasman Terrace, Port Lincoln, SA 5606
(08) 8682 2133

QUEENSLAND

BRISBANE

Cru Bar & Cellar
22 James Street, Fortitude Valley, QLD 4006
(07) 3252 1744

The Gap Tavern

21 Glenquarie Place, The Gap, QLD 4061
(07) 3366 6090
www.gaptavern.com.au

The Grape Group

85 Merthyr Road, New Farm, QLD 4005
(07) 3358 6000
www.thegrape.com.au

The Liquor Superstore

577 Settlement Road, Keperra, QLD 4054
(07) 3351 0499

The Liquor Superstore/Liquor Saver

201 Ferry Road, Southport, QLD, 4215
(07) 55565155
ferryrd@liquorstore.com

Mr Corks

Jindalee Hotel, Sinnamon Road (cnr Goggs Road),
Jindalee QLD 4074
(07) 3710 5858
www.mrcorks.com.au

Paddington Tavern

186 Given Terrace, Paddington, QLD 4064
(07) 3369 0044

Stewarts Wine Co.

Racecourse Road (cnr of Dobson Street), Ascot, QLD 4007
1800 138 838
www.stewartshomesupply.com.au

Story Bridge Hotel

200 Main Street, Kangaroo Point, QLD
(07) 3391 2266
www.storybridgehotel.com.au

The Wine Emporium

Shop 47, 1000 Ann Street, Fortitude Valley QLD 4006
(07) 3252 1117
www.thewineemporium.com.au

OUTSIDE BRISBANE

Austral Hotel
189 Victoria Street, Mackay, QLD 4740
(07) 4951 3288
www.australhotel.com.au

Barrier Reef Hotel
33 Wharf Street, Cairns, QLD 4870
(07) 4051 4245

Courthouse Hotel
51 Nerang Street, Southport, QLD
(07) 5532 0122

Seaview Hotel
56 The Strand, North Ward, QLD 4810
(07) 4771 5005

Smithfield Tavern
Captain Cook Highway, Smithfield, QLD 4878
(07) 4038 1411

Sunshine Cellars
50 Hastings Street, Noosa Heads, QLD 4567
1800 555 545

Villa Noosa Hotel
Mary Street, Noosaville, QLD 4566
(07) 5449 7766
www.villanoosa.com.au

WESTERN AUSTRALIA

PERTH

Barossa Cellars
278 Railway Parade, Leederville, WA 6007
(08) 9381 1770

Bicton Cellars
221 Preston Road, Bicton, WA 6157
(08) 9339 1917

BWS

Shop 1, 22 Culloton Crescent, Balga, WA 6061
(08) 9342 2568
www.beerwinespirit.com.au

Chateau Guildford

124 Swan Street, Guildford, WA 6055
(08) 9377 3311

Grant & Knowles

24 Railway Street, Cottesloe, WA 6011
(08) 9384 3920

Harborne & Cambridge Cellars

252 Cambridge Street, Wembley, WA 6014
(08) 9388 3033

Invinity Fine Wine Brokers

(08) 9315 3777
www.invinity.com.au

La Vigna

302 Walcott Street, Menora, WA 6050
(08) 9271 1179
www.lavigna.com.au

Liquor Barons Herdsman

Shop 5, 1 Flynn Street, Churchlands, WA 6018
(08) 9387 4222

Liquor Barons Mt Lawley

654 Beaufort Street, Mt Lawley, WA 6050
(08) 9271 0886

Liquor Barons South Perth

23 Mends Street, South Perth, WA 6050
(08) 9367 1001

Old Bridge Cellars

221 Queen Victoria Street, North Fremantle, WA 6159
(08) 9335 2702
oldbridge@iinet.net.au

Paddington Ale House

141 Scarborough Beach Road, Mt Hawthorn, WA 6016
(08) 9242 3077

Rossmoyne Cellars

5 Third Avenue, Rossmoyne, WA 6148
(08) 9457 6439

Scarborough Cellars

166 Scarborough Beach Road, Scarborough, WA 6019
(08) 9341 1437

Stephen McHenry Wine Merchants

171 Broadway, Nedlands, WA 6009
(08) 9386 3336
bottleshop@steves.com.au

Swanbourne Cellars

103 Claremont Crescent, Swanbourne, WA 6010
(08) 9384 2111
swanycellars@bigpond.com

ACT

Australian Winebrokers

21 Lonsdale Street, Braddon, ACT 2612
(02) 6262 8599
www.australianwinebrokers.com

Braddon Cellars

11 Lonsdale Street, Braddon ACT 2612
(02) 6247 2440

Campbell's Liquor Discount

4 Blamey Place, Campbell, ACT 2612
(02) 6247 1366

George's Liquor Stable

17 Dundas Court, Phillip, ACT 2606
(02) 6285 3075
74 Northbourne Avenue, Braddon, ACT 2612
(02) 6247 1377

Jim Murphy's Market Wine Cellars

19 Mildura Street, Fyshwick, ACT 2609
(02) 6295 0060

Local Liquor

Wattle Street, Lyneham, ACT 2602
(02) 6249 7263
This is one of a large group of independent retailers situated in most
parts of Canberra. For store locations, check www.localliquor.com.au

The Wine Shed

Shop 27, Belconnen Markets, Lathlain Street, Belconnen ACT 2612
(02) 6251 3781

TASMANIA

HOBART

Aberfeldy Cellars BWS

128 Davey Street, Hobart, TAS 7000
(03) 6211 6633

Gasworks 9/11 Bottleshop

Shop 3, 2 Macquarie Street, Hobart, TAS 7000
(03) 6214 7525

OUTSIDE HOBART

Alexander Hotel

79 Formby Road, Devonport, TAS 7310
(03) 6424 2252

Benchmark Tasmania Wine Gallery

135 Paterson Street, Launceston, TAS 7250
(03) 6331 3977
www.benchmarkwinegallery.com

Club Hotel

22 Mount Street, Burnie, TAS 7320
(03) 6431 2244

Gunners Arms Tavern

23 Lawrence Street, Launceston, TAS 7250
(03) 6331 3891

TRC Bottleshop
131 Paterson Street, Launceston, TAS 7250
(03) 6331 3424

NORTHERN TERRITORY

Beachfront Hotel
342 Casuarina Drive, Rapid Creek, NT 0810
(08) 8985 3000

Hidden Valley Tavern
Stuart Highway, Berrimah, NT 0828
(08) 8984 3999
info@hiddenvalleytavern.com.au

Northside Foodland
3 Hearn Place, Alice Springs, NT 0870
(08) 8952 2754

Parap Fine Foods
40 Parap Road, Parap, NT 0820
(08) 8981 8597
www.parapfinefoods.com

Parap Village Tavern
15 Parap Road, Parap, NT 0820
(08) 8981 2191
parapvillagetavern@bigpond.com

Vintage Cellars
27 Cavenagh Street, Darwin, NT 0800
(08) 8941 7345

Wine Clubs and Online Retailers

There are disadvantages to joining a direct-selling wine club such as Cellarmasters or The Wine Society – the main ones being the inability to try before you buy, and the fact that you have to take the rough with the smooth: not every wine you are sent will be a masterpiece of the vintner's art (that's one way that costs are kept so low). The same applies to buying wine over the internet. But we think the advantages outweigh the negative sides – look, for example, at the quality and exceptional value of the Cellarmasters wines we have been able to recommend in this edition.

WINE CLUBS

Cellarmasters
1800 500 260
www.cellarmasters.com.au

Liquorland Direct
1300 300 360
www.liquorlanddirect.com.au

Vintage Cellars
1300 366 084
www.vintagecellars.com.au

Wine Selectors
1300 303 307
www.wineselectors.com.au

The Wine Society
1300 723 723
www.winesociety.com.au

ONLINE STORES

The following websites often have some excellent prices, and all have a good range, including some smaller-producer, harder-to-get wines and, in many cases, a wide range of cleanskins.

www.auscellardoor.com.au

www.auswine.com.au

www.boccaccio.com.au

www.boutiquewineries.com.au

www.ckdirect.com.au

www.cleanskins.com

www.discountwines.com

www.nicks.com.au

www.organicwine.com.au

www.ozliquormart.com.au

www.prospectwines.com.au

www.tastingroom.com.au

www.winelarder.com.au

www.winepool.com.au

www.winestar.com.au

www.winezy.com.au

SEARCH ENGINES

The Wine Searcher website is very powerful and extremely useful in finding wines – and their wildly varying prices – all around the world, not just in Australia. If you buy a lot of wine online, it's worth signing up to the Pro version:

www.wine-searcher.com

And despite its limited scope, the Wine Robot search engine can return some great bargains:

www.winerobot.com.au

Decoding the jargon

A quick wine glossary

A QUICK WINE GLOSSARY

MAX ALLEN

aromatic

A catch-all phrase that refers to wines with strong positive aromas, such as the powerfully varietal smells of good sauvignon blanc.

austere

A wine that tastes a little mean, hard and tight, as though the flavours are there, but the wine doesn't want to give them to you.

bottle-aged

If wines are left alone in the bottle for a number of years, they can develop complex, savoury bottle-aged characters, quite distinct from the fresh, fruity characters they had when they were young.

buttery

Some winemaking techniques – for example, malolactic fermentation and lees contact – can contribute a rich, creamy, buttery aroma and flavour to wooded whites such as chardonnay.

chalky

Steely, flinty, minerally. The words used to describe really dry white wines.

chewy

Chewy red wines have lots of grape-skin extracts in them, giving a strong impression of being really thick and full in the mouth.

clean

Simply, a wine that is free of faults: fresh-tasting, pleasant. 'Clean' can occasionally be a more loaded description, implying that the wine is technically correct, but not overly exciting.

closed

Or dumb. A wine that tastes like a shadow of its former self. The opposite, of course, is 'open' or 'forward': a wine that seems to be wearing all its flavours on its sleeve and showing off a bit.

coarse

Wine that's a bit unsubtle and rough-tasting is 'coarse' – a bit too dry, a bit too sharp. 'Unbalanced' might be more correct; 'rustic' might be more diplomatic.

complex

You take a sniff and smell blackberries. You take another sniff and smell cherries. Another and wet undergrowth. Another and just a hint of fresh cracked pepper. This is a complex wine.

dusty

The tannins in young red wines can give a bizarre impression of being dry and dusty along the sides and back of your tongue.

elegant

A word you see a lot on wine labels. It means exactly what it says: the wine is balanced, tastes fine, is pleasing – all without knocking your tastebuds around.

fat

A wine that fills every corner of your mouth and sits plumply, but perhaps a little clumsily, on your tongue.

faults

Things can go wrong with wine at any stage, from when the grapes are picked to when the bottle is opened. The symptoms and causes of the most common faults are listed below. If you find them in your wine, you have every right to complain, send back the bottle to the waiter, or ask for an exchange from the bottleshop.

fault 1: hazy appearance

In wines that should be crystal clear – like young riesling, for example – cloudiness can indicate bacterial spoilage.

fault 2: dull, brown colour

The wine has come into contact with too much oxygen due to a leaky cork, has oxidised and is on its way to becoming vinegar. This is more relevant for white wine.

fault 3: musty, mouldy smells

Occasionally caused by the wine being stored in dirty, old barrels, but most often a musty smell is caused by cork taint. Cork is prone to all kinds of contamination which can, in turn, taint the wine, making it taste 'corked' – flat, dull, even quite rank – like mouldy cardboard.

fault 4: smells like rotten eggs or burnt matches

Rotten eggs is hydrogen sulphide, which can form in a wine during fermentation. It is usually easily dealt with by the winemaker, but occasionally creeps into the bottle. Burnt match smells are due to excessive sulphur dioxide, which is a preservative added to most wines.

fault 5: vinegary or solvent smells

These come from excessive levels of volatile acids (known as VA), and/or ethyl acetate. The volatile acids (such as the vinegar acid, acetic acid) are the ones we can smell. Ethyl acetate is formed when acetic acid combines with alcohol. A little VA can add complexity and lift the aromas of a wine; a lot can make it smell like nail-polish remover.

'fault' 6: tiny, crunchy crystals in the bottle

You can come across these in sweet white wines and older red wines. They are *not a fault*, but natural tartrate crystals that can develop when the wine ages or gets too cold. They do not affect the wine's taste or quality.

finish

The aftertaste. As in: 'This full-bodied shiraz has an extraordinarily long finish that lingers in the mouth for a minute.' As with so much else in life, the longer the better, obviously.

firm

Solid, taut, tense, sturdy – a more pleasant version of 'austere'.

fleshy

A more positive way of saying 'fat': a wine with plenty of palpable fruit in the mouth.

floral

Literally, smelling like flowers.

full-bodied

A wine that fills the mouth and seems to impose on the palate – in contrast with medium- and light-bodied wines, which make a less imposing impression.

green or herbaceous

There are two main reasons why a wine might smell grassy, herbaceous or green. It's either meant to – like sauvignon blanc – or the grapes that made it were under-ripe – like some red wines grown in very cool climates.

hot

Wine made from over-ripe grapes grown in warm climates can produce a hot-tasting burn of alcohol at the back of the throat. The fruit in those wines can also taste a bit jammy.

lifted

Sometimes the delicate, spicy or fragrant aromas in a wine seem to be lifted towards your nose by some invisible hand.

long

A very good thing. A wine that has a long finish is one whose flavours seem to go on and on and on for seconds, right down the back of your throat.

nose

How the wine smells. As in: 'This young chardonnay has a marvellous nose of apples, vanilla and oatmeal.' If you're feeling posh, you could use the word 'bouquet'.

nutty

Sometimes wines can taste nutty because of the barrels they're stored in (chardonnay, for example), and sometimes it's a flavour found in the grape variety they're made from (pinot gris).

oaky or woody

Again, a catch-all term that covers all sorts of descriptions from the vanilla-like smell of new oak barrels used to age the wine before bottling to the cedarwood smell of old cabernet, and also covering the toasty smells, the spicy smells, the dusty smells and even the dirty old barrel smells.

rich

Wine with lots of viscosity, flesh, substance and fruit.

smoky

Some white grapes such as gewürztraminer and pinot gris can make wines with a dusky, smoky perfume; and sometimes barrels can give wine that's stored in them a different, more pungent, smoky or charred aroma.

spicy

Like smoky aromas, spicy characters can come from the grape varieties (the pepperiness of shiraz, for example) or the barrel (the clove and aniseed aromas of some –French – oak).

stalky

A little stalkiness (in wines that have been fermented with a few of the grape stems included) can be a good, complex thing. A lot just makes the wine taste green and stalky.

tannic

Tannins are the astringent bit of grape skins. Grapes with thick skins and lots of tannin like cabernet can produce 'tannic' wine, which tastes particularly dry and savoury, as if the liquid is gripping onto your tongue and gums before you swallow.

thin

The opposite of fat, and hardly ever a good thing. Thin wines, wines that are really neutral-tasting, that seem hollow and lean, are usually the result of overcropped grapes and poor winemaking.

varietal

Literally, tastes like the grape variety the wine was made from.

zingy

Crisp, fresh, lively, juicy, tangy, zesty, lemony, citrusy – these are all good words for wines with noticeable but pleasant acidity. 'Sharp' and 'sour' are used when the acid's unbalanced and unpleasant.

Index of wines

Alkoomi Shiraz Viognier 181
All Saints Golden Cream Sherry 154
All Saints Rutherglen Muscat 194
All Saints Rutherglen Tokay 194
Andrew Garrett Cabernet Merlot 122
Andrew Garrett Chardonnay 47
Andrew Garrett 'Garrett' Brut 31
Andrew Garrett 'Garrett' Semillon
   Chardonnay 74
Andrew Garrett 'Garrett' Shiraz Cabernet
   135
Andrew Garrett Pinot Noir Chardonnay 30
Andrew Garrett Shiraz 110
Andrew Garrett Sparkling Burgundy 34
Angas Brut 31
Angove's 'Anchorage' Old Tawny 153
Angove's 'Bookmark' Marsala 156
Angove's 'Nine Vines' Rosé 92
Angove's 'Stonegate' Petit Verdot 118
Angove's 'Stonegate' Unwooded
   Chardonnay 43
Angove's 'Stonegate' Verdelho 69
Angove's 'Bear Crossing' Chardonnay 45
Angove's 'Butterfly Ridge' Colombard
   Chadonnay 85
Angove's 'Butterfly Ridge' Riesling 53
Angove's 'Butterfly Ridge' Spaetlese Lexia
   146
Angove's 'Paddle Wheel' Muscat 24
Angove's 'Red Belly Black' Shiraz 113
Angus the Bull Cabernet Sauvignon 96
Annie's Lane Riesling 54
Arakoon 'Lighthouse' Cabernet Sauvignon
   181
Asti Riccadonna, 160
Australian Old Vine 'Sovereign Wine'
   Chambourcin 118

Baileys 'Founder' Port 195
Balnaves Cabernet Sauvignon 181
Balnaves Chardonnay 173
Banrock Station Cabernet Merlot 22
Banrock Station Pinot Noir Chardonnay 29
Banrock Station Shiraz Cabernet Sauvignon
   22
Banrock Station The Reserve Sparkling
   Shiraz 33
Banrock Station White Shiraz 19
Barking Owl Shiraz 182
Barrecas Barbera 119
Barrecas Shiraz Malbec 182
Barwang Cabernet Sauvignon 182
Barwick Estate 'St Johns Brook'
   Chardonnay 47
Bay of Fires 'Tigress' Rosé 179
Beelgara Estate Black '15.03' Shiraz 113
Beelgara Estate '11.05' Pinot Grigio 67
Beelgara Estate 'Silky Oak' Semillon
   Chardonnay 74

Beelgara Estate 'Silky Oak' Shiraz 107
(La) Belle Terrasse Shiraz, France 165
Beresford 'Highwood' Merlot 100
Beresford 'Highwood' Sauvignon Blanc 60
Bethany 'Select' Late Harvest Riesling 194
Bethany Semillon 64
Bimbadgen Ridge Sparkling Semillon 30
Bleasdale Chardonnay 48
Bleasdale Malbec 117
Bleasdale Shiraz Cabernet 135
Bleasdale Verdelho 70
Blue Pyrenees 'Summer' Rosé 179
Blues Point Chardonnay Semillon 74
Bowen Estate Shiraz 182
Brands Cabernet Sauvignon 182
Broken Earth Cabernet Merlot 123
Broomstick Estate Shiraz 183
Brown Brothers Dry Red 22
Brown Brothers Fruity White 19
Brown Brothers Merlot 183
Brown Brothers Moscato 36
Brown Brothers Orange Muscat & Flora 148
Brown Brothers Pinot Grigio 173
Brown Brothers Pinot Grigio 69
Brown Brothers Reserve Muscat 195
Brown Brothers Reserve Port 152
Brown Brothers Spatlese Lexia 146
Brown Brothers Tarrango 120
Browns of Padthaway Unwooded
   Chardonnay 42
Buckland Gap Cabernet Merlot 126
Buckland Gap Traminer Riesling 146
Buller 'Victoria' Muscat 155
Buller 'Caspia' Chardonnay 48
Buller Fine Old Tokay 195
Buller 'Victoria' Tawny 153
Buller 'Victoria' Tokay 155

Campbells Rutherglen Muscat 195
Cantine Rallo 'Spirita di Rallo' Nero d'Avola
   Cabernet 165
Cape Mentelle 'Georgiana' 84
Cape Mentelle 'Marmaduke' 183
Cape Schanck Pinot Noir 119
Capel Vale 'CV' Cabernet Merlot 126
Capel Vale 'CV' Semillon Sauvignon Blanc
   173
Capel Vale 'CV' Unwooded Chardonnay 43
Capel Vale 'CV' Sauvignon Blanc 59
Capel Vale Duck 90
Carrington Blush 35
Carrington Brut Reserve 31
Cartwheel Sauvignon Blanc Semillon 78
Castello di Gabbiano Chianti 166
Cerro del Masso Chianti 166
Chain of Ponds 'Novello Bianco' Semillon
   Pinot Grigio 85
Chain of Ponds 'Novello' Nero 131
Chain of Ponds 'Novello' Rosso 131

Charles Melton 'Rosé of Virginia' 179
Chateau Tanunda 'Barossa Tower' Shiraz 183
Chateau Tanunda 'Barossa Tower' Moscato 37
Chestnut Grove 'Tall Timber' Shiraz Cabernet 134
Cheviot Bridge 'CB' Cabernet Merlot 125
Cheviot Bridge 'CB' Heathcote Shiraz 108
Chrismont Riesling 54
Cleanskin Reserve RP04 Sparkling Pinot Noir Chardonnay 32
Clovely Estate 'Left Field' Verdelho 71
Cockatoo Ridge Cabernet Merlot 126
Coldstream Hills Merlot 183
Cookoothama Chardonnay 46
Cookoothama Shiraz 110
Coolabah Fresh Dry White 19
Cora Asti 160
Coriole '8 Gauge' Cabernet Merlot 126
Coriole Chenin Blanc 69
Coriole 'Contour 4' Sangiovese Shiraz 141
Cowra Estate Cabernets Rosé 91
Crocodile Creek 'Undercurrent' 85
Crofters Semillon Sauvignon Blanc 81
Cumulus 'Rolling' Cabernet Merlot 124
Cumulus 'Climbing' Merlot 184

Dal Broi 'Red Hill' Cabernet Shiraz Merlot 140
Dal Broi 'Yarranvale Station' Cabernet Merlot 126
Dal Broi 'Yarranvale Station' Chardonnay 48
D'Arenberg 'The Cadenzia' Grenache Shiraz Mourvedre 184
D'Arenberg 'The Footbolt' Shiraz 184
D'Arenberg 'The Stump Jump' Grenache Shiraz Mourvedre 131
De Bortoli 'Black Creek' Cabernet Merlot 126
De Bortoli 'Black Creek' Shiraz 110
De Bortoli 'Deen Vat 7' Chardonnay 45
De Bortoli 'Deen Vat 8' Shiraz 113
De Bortoli 'Deen Vat 9' Cabernet Sauvignon 97
De Bortoli 'Emeri' Sparkling Durif 34
De Bortoli Premium Reserve Merlot 21
De Bortoli Premium Reserve Shiraz 21
De Bortoli Premium Semillon Trebbiano Chardonnay 19
De Bortoli 'Sacred Hill' Cabernet Merlot 123
De Bortoli 'Windy Peak' Cabernet Shiraz Merlot 141
De Bortoli 'Windy Peak' Pinot Noir Chardonnay 35
De Bortoli 'Windy Peak' Sangiovese 117
Deakin Estate Cabernet Sauvignon 98
Deakin Estate Shiraz 110
Deakin Estate Rosé 91

Deutz Marlborough Brut Cuvee 160
Domaine du Tariquet Cotes du Gascogne Ugni Blanc Colombard 164
Domaines Perrin La Vieille Ferme Cotes du Ventoux Rosé 166
Domaines Perrin La Vieille Ferme 'Lasira' 165
Dowie Doole Chenin Blanc 70

Elderton 'Ashmead Family' Sauvignon Blanc Verdelho 85
Elderton Unwooded Chardonnay 42
Evans & Tate 'Gnangara' Chenin Blanc 70
Evans & Tate ''Gnangara' Merlot 104
Evans & Tate 'Gnangara' Sauvignon Blanc 60
Evans & Tate 'Gnangara' Unwooded Chardonnay 42
Evans & Tate Margaret River Chardonnay 173
Evans & Tate Margaret River Sauvignon Blanc Semillon 81
Evans & Tate 'Salisbury' Cabernet Merlot 125

Ferngrove Cabernet Merlot 125
Ferngrove 'Majestic' Cabernet Sauvignon 184
Ferngrove Sauvignon Blanc Semillon 80
Fiddlers Creek Shiraz Cabernet 134
Fishbone Cabernet Shiraz 135
Fishbone Classic White 84
Fishers Circle Shiraz Merlot Cabernet Sauvignon 140
Flying Fish Cove Shiraz 184
Four Sisters Pinot Noir Chardonnay 32
Four Sisters Sauvignon Blanc Semillon 78
Fox Creek 'Shadows Run' Shiraz Cabernet 135
Fox River Cabernet Shiraz 134
Fox River Shiraz 108

Galah Riesling 54
Gapsted 'Victorian Alps' Moscato 37
Gapsted Ballerina Canopy Sauvignon Blanc 174
Gapsted Chardonnay 48
Gapsted 'Victorian Alps' Dolcetto Syrah 140
Gemtree 'Uncut' Shiraz 184
Geoff Merrill 'Liquid Asset' Shiraz Grenache 131
Geoff Merrill Shiraz Grenache Mourvedre 130
Gilberts 'Three Devil's' Shiraz 185
Glaetzer 'Wallace' Shiraz Cabernet Grenache 185
Goundrey 'Homestead' Riesling 52
Goundrey 'Homestead' Sauvignon Blanc Semillon 81
Gramps Shiraz 185
Grandin Brut, France 160
Grandin Rosé 161

Hamiltons Ewell 'Sturt River' Chardonnay 45
Hardys 'Oomoo' Shiraz 108
Hardys Regional Reserve Classic Cuvee Pink 35
Hardys Shiraz 21
Hardys 'Sir James' Pinot Noir Chardonnay 172
Hardys Vintage Port 195
Hardys 'Whiskers Blake' Port 152
Haselgrove Shiraz 113
Hazard Hill Semillon Sauvignon Blanc 81
Heartland 'Stickleback' Cabernet Shiraz Grenache 129
Heemskerk Pinot Noir Chardonnay 172
Heritage Semillon 62
Houghton Cabernet Sauvignon 98
Houghton Cabernet Shiraz Merlot 140
Houghton Chardonnay 46
Houghton Chardonnay Verdelho 85
Houghton Chenin Blanc 67
Houghton Semillon Sauvignon Blanc 79
Houghton White Burgundy 86

Jacobs Creek Brut Cuvee Chardonnay Pinot Noir 32
Jacobs Creek Reserve Riesling 54
Jacobs Creek Reserve Shiraz 109
Jacobs Creek Shiraz 113
Jacobs Creek Shiraz Rosé 91
Jamiesons Run Cabernet Sauvignon 96
Jamiesons Run Sauvignon Blanc 60
Jamiesons Run Shiraz 110
Jane Brook 'Plain Jane' Rosé 92
Jean Pierre & Co. Celebration Brut 32
Jim Barry 'Lavender Hill' Riesling 146
Jim Barry Watervale Riesling 52
Jingalla Cabernet Rouge 91
Jip Jip Rocks Shiraz 111
Juniper Crossing Cabernet Sauvignon 185
Juniper Crossing Semillon Sauvignon Blanc 174

Kaiser Stuhl Crisp Dry White 18
Kangaroo Ridge 'The Aussie' White Shiraz 90
Kilikanoon 'Killerman's Run' Shiraz 185
Kilikanoon 'Killermans Run' Shiraz Grenache 186
Kilikanoon Rosé 179
Kingston Estate Cabernet Merlot 126
Kingston Estate Cabernet Sauvignon 98
Kingston Estate Sauvignon Blanc 60
Kingston Estate Verdelho 71
Kirrihill Estates 'Companions' Cabernet Merlot 125
Kirrihill Estates 'Companions' Chardonnay 46
Knappstein 'Three' 174
Kooyong 'Massale' Pinot Noir 186

Leaping Lizard Semillon Sauvignon Blanc 79
Leasingham 'Bastion' Riesling 56
Leasingham 'Bin 7' Riesling 175
Lillydale Rosé 179
Lillypilly Lexia 146
Lilyvale Semillon 65
Lindauer Fraise 161
Lindeaur Special Reserve 160
Lindemans 'Bin 35' Rosé 92
Lindemans 'Bin 40' Merlot 104
Lindemans 'Bin 45' Cabernet Sauvignon 97
Lindemans 'Bin 55' Shiraz Cabernet 136
Lindemans 'Cawarra' Cabernet Merlot 125
Lindemans 'Cawarra' Cabernet Merlot 22
Lindemans 'Cawarra' Chardonnay 19
Lindemans 'Cawarra' Merlot 104
Lindemans 'Cawarra' Semillon Chardonnay 74
Lindemans 'Cawarra' Shiraz Cabernet 135
Lindemans Premium Varietal Chardonnay 19
Lindemans Reserve Cabernet Merlot 124
Lindemans Reserve Pinot Noir Chardonnay Pinot Meunier 30
Lindemans Reserve Shiraz 111
Lindemans Reserve Verdelho 70
Little Brother Shiraz Cabernet 186
Little Penguin Chardonnay 46
Little Penguin Shiraz 111
Logan 'Apple Tree Flat' Chardonnay 44
Logan 'Apple Tree Flat' Semillon Sauvignon Blanc 80
Logan 'Weemala' Merlot 102
Long Flat Cabernet Merlot 127
Long Flat Semillon Sauvignon Blanc 80
Long Flat Wine Company Chardonnay 44
Long Flat Wine Company Pinot Noir 117
Long Flat Wine Company Sauvignon Blanc 59

M Chapoutier 'Bila Haut' Cotes de Roussillon 166
Madfish Riesling 175
Majella Cabernet Sauvignon 187
Majella 'The Musician' Cabernet Shiraz 187
Masi 'Levarie' Soave, Italy 162
Matthew Lang Semillon Chardonnay 74
McGuigan Bin 9000 Semillon 63
McGuigan 'Black Label' Verdelho 71
McPherson Cabernet Sauvignon 98
McPherson Chardonnay 48
McPherson Semillon Sauvignon Blanc 80
McPherson Verdelho 71
McWilliams 'Hanwood' Amontillado Sherry 154
McWilliams 'Hanwood' Chardonnay 48
McWilliams 'Hanwood' Classic Muscat 155
McWilliams 'Hanwood' Classic Tawny 153
McWilliams 'Hanwood' Merlot 101

McWilliams 'Hanwood' Pinot Noir Chardonnay 32
McWilliams 'Hanwood' Shiraz 111
McWilliams 'Hanwood' Oloroso Sherry 154
McWilliams 'Inheritance' Cabernet Merlot 127
McWilliams 'Inheritance' Fruitwood 147
McWilliams 'Inheritance' Riesling 56
McWilliams 'Inheritance' Semillon Sauvignon Blanc 81
McWilliams 'Inheritance' Shiraz Cabernet 136
McWilliams 'Regional Collection' Clare Valley Riesling 54
Mildara Chestnut Teal Oloroso 154
Mildara Rio Vista Dry Sherry 154
Mildara Supreme Dry Sherry 154
Minchinbury Fine Private Cuvee 35
Minot Cabernet Sauvignon 187
Mistletoe Reserve Chardonnay 175
Mitchelton 'Blackwood Park' Riesling 54
Mitchelton 'Preece' Sauvignon Blanc 60
Mitchelton 'Preece' Shiraz 111
Mondoro Asti 161
Montana 'Reserve' Chardonnay 162
Montana 'Reserve' Pinot Noir 167
Montana 'Reserve' Sauvignon Blanc 175
Montana Sauvignon Blanc 162
Moondah Brook Cabernet Rosé 92
Moondah Brook Verdelho 68
Moondah Brook Verdelho 71
Morambro Creek Unwooded Chardonnay 43
Morris Black Label Liqueur Muscat 155
Morris Cabernet Sauvignon 98
Morris Liqueur Tokay 196
Mount Hurtle Grenache Rosé 92
Mount Majura Chardonnay 176
Mount Majura Pinot Gris 176
Mount Pleasant 'Elizabeth' Semillon 63
Mount Riley Pinot Noir 167
Mount Riley Sauvignon Blanc 163
Mount Trio Sauvignon Blanc 59
Mr Riggs Shiraz Viognier 187

Nepenthe 'Tryst' Sauvignon Blanc Semillon 79
Nepenthe 'Tryst' Cabernet Tempranillo Zinfandel 139
Ninth Island Chardonnay 176
Normanno Inzolia 164
Nova 'Tickled Pink' Rosé 37
Nugan Estate Shiraz 187

O'Leary Walker Shiraz 188
Omni 30
Omni Blue 36
Omni Pink 35
Omni Red 34
Oyster Bay Merlot 166

Palandri 'Baldivis' Classic Dry White 84
Palandri 'Baldivis' Merlot 104
Palandri Riesling 56
Palandri Semillon Sauvignon Blanc 176
Parri Semillon 65
Paul Conti 'Fronti' Muscat 146
Paul Conti Grenache Shiraz 130
Paul Conti 'Medici Ridge' Merlot 102
Paul Conti 'The Tuarts' Chenin Blanc 71
Pauletts Shiraz 188
Penfolds Club Reserve Aged Tawny 152
Penfolds Club Tawny 153
Penfolds 'Koonunga Hill' Semillon Chardonnay 75
Penfolds 'Koonunga Hill' Semillon Sauvignon Blanc 81
Penfolds 'Rawsons Retreat' Chardonnay 48
Penfolds 'Rawsons Retreat' Merlot 101
Penfolds 'Rawsons Retreat' Riesling 56
Penfolds 'Wood Aged' 24
Penfolds 'Wood Aged' Port 24
Pepperjack Grenache Rosé 179
Pertaringa Final Fronti 147
Petaluma 'Hanelin Hill' Riesling 177
Peter Lehmann Barossa Riesling 55
Peter Lehmann Chardonnay 46
Peter Lehmann 'Clancy's' Shiraz Cabernet Merlot 140
Peter Lehmann Eden Valley Riesling 53
Peter Lehmann Grenache Shiraz Mourvedre 130
Peter Lehmann Merlot 102
Peter Lehmann Semillon 64
Peter Lehmann Semillon Chardonnay 74
Peter Lehmann Shiraz Grenache 131
Pewsey Vale Riesling 55
Pikes 'Luccio' Sangiovese Cabernet Petit Verdot 139
Pillar Box Red Cabernet Shiraz Merlot 139
Poets Corner Shiraz Cabernet 136
Pol Gessner 172
Potters Clay Shiraz 188
Primo Estate 'La Biondina' 85
Prunotto Barbera d'Alba 181
Pump Hill Semillon Chardonnay 75
Punt Road Chardonnay 177
Punt Road Merlot 188

Queen Adelaide Cabernet Merlot 124
Queen Adelaide Cabernet Sauvignon 97
Queen Adelaide Chardonnay 20
Queen Adelaide Classic Dry White 86
Queen Adelaide Merlot 104
Queen Adelaide Riesling 53
Queen Adelaide Shiraz 113

Red Deer Station Cabernet Sauvignon 98
Red Deer Station Merlot 103

Red Deer Station Semillon Chardonnay 74
Red Deer Station Unoaked Shiraz 113
Redbank 'Fighting Flat' Shiraz 188
Redbank 'Long Paddock' Merlot 105
Richmond Grove Riesling 177
Richmond Grove Watervale Riesling 177
Roberts Estate Cabernet Sauvignon 96
Roberts Estate Merlot 105
Roberts Estate Shiraz 113
Rockbare Shiraz 189
Rockfield Semillon 178
Rosemount Estate 'Diamond Label'
    Cabernet Merlot 125
Rosemount Estate 'Diamond Label'
    Grenache Shiraz 129
Rosemount Estate 'Diamond Label' Merlot
    105
Rosemount Estate 'Diamond Label' Pinot
    Noir 120
Rosemount Estate 'Diamond Label'
    Riesling 56
Rosemount Estate 'Diamond Label'
    Semillon 64
Rosemount Estate Diamond Label'
    Semillon Chardonnay 73
Rosemount Estate 'Diamond Label' Shiraz
    109
Rosemount Estate 'Diamond Label' Shiraz
    Grenache Viognier 131
Rosemount Estate 'Diamond Label'
    Traminer Riesling 146
Rosemount Estate 'Jigsaw' Riesling Fronti
    Verdelho 84
Rosemount Estate 'Jigsaw' Shiraz Mataro
    Grenache 130
Rossetto Brothers Tawny Port 152
Rouge Homme Cabernet Merlot 127
Rouge Homme Cabernet Sauvignon 97
Ruffino 'Lumina del Borgo ' Pinot Grigio
    163
Rutherglen Estates 'Red' Shiraz Durif 141
Rutherglen Estates 'The Reunion'
    Mourvedre Shiraz Grenache 141

Saint Clair Pinot Noir 189
Saltram 'Makers Table' Semillon 65
Saltram 'Makers Table' Shiraz 112
Saltram 'Next Chapter' Cab Merlot 189
Saltram 'Next Chapter' Cabernet Merlot 127
Saltram 'Next Chapter' Shiraz 112
Sandalford 'Element' Chardonnay 44
Sandalford 'Element' Classic White 86
Sandalford 'Element' Merlot 103
Sarantos Chardonnay 48
Sarantos Merlot 105
Scarpantoni 'Block 3' Shiraz 189
Scarpantoni 'Ceres' Rosé 90
Scarpantoni 'Pedler Creek' Cabernet
    Sauvignon 97

Scarpantoni 'Pedler Creek' Merlot 103
Scarpantoni 'Pedler Creek' Sangiovese 120
Scarpantoni 'School Block' Shiraz Cabernet
    Merlot 142
Schild Estate Frontignac 147
Seaview Brut de Brut 32
Seaview Grande Cuvee 31
Selaks Sauvignon Blanc 163
Seppelt 'Chalambar' Shiraz 190
Seppelt DP 57 Grand Tokay 196
Seppelt Great Western Brut Reserve 31
Seppelt Great Western Imperial Reserve 31
Seppelt Medium Dry Sherry 24
Seppelt Para 123 Liqueur Tawny 196
Seppelt 'Solero' Cream Sherry 24
Seppelt 'Victoria' Cabernet Sauvignon 190
Seppelt 'Victoria' Shiraz 190
Siegersdorf Riesling 55
Simon Gilbert Card Collection Chardonnay
    45
Sir James Pinot Noir Chardonnay 29
Sir James Sparkling Pinot Noir Shiraz 33
Sirromet Verdelho 71
Six Foot Six Pinot Noir 191
Skillogalee Riesling 178
Skuttlebutt Cabernet Shiraz Merlot 191
Snowy Creek Chenin Blanc Verdelho 86
Solo Arte Sangiovese 167
St Hallett 'Gamekeepers' Reserve 130
St Hallett 'Blackwell' Shiraz 189
Sticks Chardonnay 46
Sticks Pinot Noir 118
Sticks Yarra Valley Merlot 103
Stonehaven 'Stepping Stone' Shiraz 109
Stoneleigh Sauvignon Blanc 164
Stones Green Ginger Wine 156
Stonleigh Marlborough Pinot Noir 167

Tahbilk Marsanne 68
Tall Poppy 'Hillside' Petit Verdot 119
Tall Poppy Merlot 105
Tall Poppy Merlot Cabernet Shiraz 142
Tall Poppy 'Select' Rosé 92
Tall Poppy 'Select' Shiraz 113
Tall Poppy Shiraz 114
Tamar Ridge 'Devil's Corner' Pinot Noir 191
Taylors 'Promised Land' White Cabernet 91
Taylors Merlot 101
Taylors 'Promised Land' Shiraz Cabernet 136
Taylors 'Promised Land' Unwooded
    Chardonnay 43
Taylors Riesling 53
Tempus Two Tempranillo 120
Terra Felix Chardonnay 47
Terra Felix Shiraz Viognier 112
T'Gallant 'Juliet' Pinot Grigio 70
T'Gallant Moscato 194
Tinja Sangiovese Merlot 191
Tobacco Road Cabernet Sauvignon 97

Tobacco Road Rosé 92
Tobacco Road Unwooded Chardonnay 43
Tollana Botrytis Riesling 148
Torbreck Woodcutters Red 192
Torres Vina Esmeralda, 163
Torzi Matthews Riesling 178
Tosti Moscato d'Asti, 161
Trentham Estate Cabernet Merlot 126
Trentham Estate Chardonnay 47
Trentham Estate 'La Famiglia' Moscato 37
Trentham Estate 'La Famiglia' Pinot Grigio 68
Trentham Estate 'Murphy's Lore'
    Chardonnay 49
Trentham Estate Shiraz 114
Tulloch Semillon 64
Turkey Flat Rosé 180
Twin Islands Pinot Noir 167
Two Hands 'Brilliant Disguise' Moscato 36
Tyrrells 'Lost Block' Cabernet Sauvignon 98
Tyrrells 'Old Winery' Semillon 65
Tyrrells 'Rufus Stone' Heathcote Shiraz 192
Tyrrells Sparkling Cabernet Sauvignon 34
Tyrrells Verdelho 71

Umani Ronchi 'Villa Bianchi ' Verdicchio 164
Upper Reach Unwooded Chardonnay 43

Vidal Fleury Cotes du Ventoux 167
Voyager Estate Shiraz 192

Wangolina Station Sauvignon Blanc 59
Westend Estate 'Outback' Shiraz 112
Westend Estate 'Richland' Sauvignon Blanc
    60
Westend Estate 'Richland' Shiraz 114
White Island Semillon Sauvignon Blanc 164
Wildfly Cabernet Merlot 127
Wirra Wirra 'Mrs Wigley' Rosé 180
Wolf Blass 'Eaglehawk' Cuvee Brut 32
Wolf Blass 'Eaglehawk' Riesling 53
Wolf Blass 'Gold Label' Cabernet Sauvignon
    Cabernet Franc 192
Wolf Blass 'Gold Label' Chardonnay 178
Wolf Blass 'Gold Label' Shiraz Viognier 192
Wolf Blass 'Red Label' Tawny Port 153
Wolf Blass 'Yellow Label' Cabernet
    Sauvignon 96
Wolf Blass 'Yellow Label' Chardonnay 47
Wolf Blass 'Yellow Label' Riesling 56

Wolf Blass 'Yellow Label' Shiraz 112
Woodlands Cabernet Merlot 193
Woop Woop 'Black Chook' Shiraz 172
Woop Woop Shiraz 110
Woop Woop Verdelho 68
Wyndham Estate 'Bin 444' Cabernet
    Sauvignon 98
Wyndham Estate 'Bin 888' Cabernet Merlot
    127
Wynns Coonawarra Riesling 55

Xabregas Unwooded Chardonnay 42

Yalumba Classic Dry Red 23
Yalumba Colombard Chardonnay 20
Yalumba 'Galway Vintage' Shiraz 114
Yalumba 'Oxford Landing' Cabernet Shiraz
    136
Yalumba 'Oxford Landing' Chardonnay 49
Yalumba Reserve Selection Cabernet
    Sauvignon 23
Yalumba Reserve Selection Cabernet Shiraz
    23
Yalumba Reserve Selection Chardonnay 18
Yalumba Reserve Selection Sauvignon
    Blanc Semillon 18
Yalumba Reserve Selection Shiraz 22
Yalumba Spatlese Fruity White 19
Yalumba 'Y Series' Merlot 102
Yalumba 'Y Series' Unwooded Chardonnay
    43
Yalumba 'Y Series' Viognier 68
Yangarra Grenache Shiraz Mourvedre 193
Yellow Tail Semillon Sauvignon Blanc 81
Yellow Tail Shiraz 114
Yellowglen 'Yellow' 29
Yering Station 'Mr Frog' Pinot Noir 120

Zilzie 'Buloke Reserve' Classic Dry White 86
Zilzie Cabernet Merlot Petit Verdot 141
Zilzie Chardonnay 47
Zilzie Petit Verdot 119
Zilzie Sangiovese 118
Zilzie Tempranillo 119
Zilzie Merlot 104
Zilzie Unwooded Chardonnay 43
Zilzie Viognier 69
Zonte's Footstep Verdelho 70
Zonte's Footsteps Cabernet Malbec 140

Now you can
Quaff ONLINE!

The Quaffing experience doesn't have to end when you put this book down.

To receive weekly reviews of great-value wines throughout the year, **subscribe for free** at

www.quaff.com.au

and hear from us each Friday with our Wine of the Week.

We'll keep you informed throughout the year as the best wines under $15 hit the market.

Don't forget to tell your friends, and Quaff on!